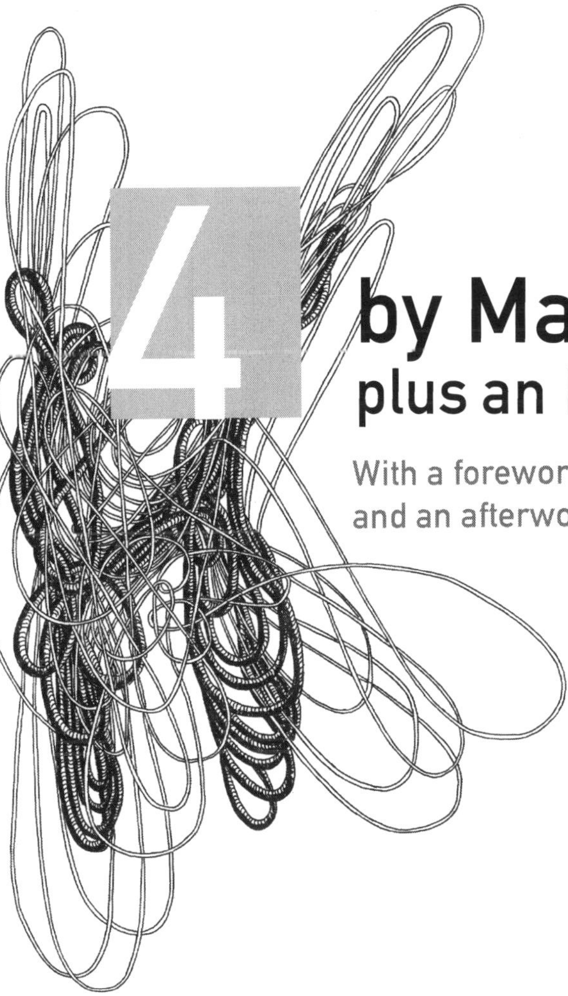

4 by Malpede plus an Intervention

With a foreword by Marvin Carlson
and an afterword by Lydia Koniordou

Egret playwrights
Chapel Hill, North Carolina
2025

Cover and book design by Maxine Mills

Printed in the United States of America
First Edition

PUBLISHER CATALOGING-IN-PUBLICATION DATA
Names: Malpede, Karen – author.
Carlson, Marvin – author of foreword.
Koniordou, Lydia – author of afterword.
Plays. Selections.
Title: 4 by Malpede plus an intervention / with a foreword by Marvin Carlson and an afterword by Lydia Koniordou.

Description: Chapel Hill : Laertes Press, 2025.
Other titles: Dramatic works. Selections. English.
Identifiers: LCCN 2025945387 | ISBN 9781942281450 (softcover : alk. paper)
Classification: LCC PS3563.A4333 A6 2025

www.laertesbooks.org

CONTENTS

A METAMORPHOSIS FOR THE TWENTY-FIRST CENTURY

By Marvin Carlson

As I read this ambitious new collection of challenging explorations of the human, non-human, and post-human works by the ever-innovative Karen Malpede, I was reminded, not for the first time but more sharply than ever, of one of the most innovative and ambitious of the classic authors, Ovid, who introduced his greatest work, the *Metamorphoses,* with a phrase that I would argue could with equal accuracy introduce a collection of Malpede's works. The Thomas Riley Gutenberg translation of Ovid begins: "My design leads me to speak of forms changed into new bodies." The necessity, indeed the inevitability, of change, along with its difficulty and dynamics, may be said to provide the driving force for each play in the present collection, as it does for much of Malpede's work. Of the four full works collected here, the two most Ovidian in their frank embrace of the symbolic, the fanciful, and the mutability of forms and bodies are clearly the two futuristic and visionary plays: *Better People*, created in 1989, and *Other Than We*, from 2018.

Before discussing them, I would like to open with a few comments on the more realistic *Us* from 1987 and *Blue Valiant*, from 2021, less obviously Ovidian in both structure and imagery, but still deeply involved, each in its own way, with the dynamics of change and its central relationship to the life process. *Us* is the darkest and cruelest of these four plays, depicting through the historical lens of the late 20th century the divided and destructive condition of the modern world. It is performed by two actors, a man and a woman, who portray a variety of characters — husband and wife, parent and child — but in every combination (including the switching of genders and the introduction of dreams) they find themselves trapped in an endless cycle of division and violence, apparently as intractable as genetic composition. These dark forces seem built into all human relationships — even the most basic, like male and female, or parent and child. The powerful and stunning opening of the play makes this point in one theatrical coup after another. We begin with a scene all too familiar in our society, a man brutally beating and verbally abusing his wife (represented here by a dummy). His rage spent, he weeps over her in remorse, then removes his clothes to reveal himself as a woman. She then introduces herself as the daughter of this suffering pair and immediately resumes the abuse of her "mother" begun by her "father."

It would be difficult to imagine a more effective and theatrical way to demonstrate the interrelatedness of gender, genetics, generational tensions, and violence in human society. Nor does this concern remain on the largely personal level. The suffering of these protagonists, we soon realize, is part of a seemingly endless cycle, the infernal machine of history that replicates their personal sufferings on a social level. Behind the central figure of Hannah, who opens the play, lie the horrors of the Holocaust and indeed the suffering of her ancestors from Abraham onward. She was, she suggests, "born of ash." Her lover Michael grew up surrounded by the atrocities of the seemingly endless Algerian war and is haunted by the vision of streets filled with disconnected body parts, the results of that protracted and devastating conflict. Like these grisly parts, the human products of this cruel and violent world seem doomed to a condition of isolation and fragmentation. As Michael informs Hannah, "I cannot attach myself to anyone."

What makes *Us* particularly dark is that although its characters are well aware of the pain and emptiness of their existences, they see no possibility of change. Their articulations of their conditions suggest no hope for the future but are best what the existentialists called creative expressions of despair. A more hopeful exploration of the human condition is offered in *Blue Valiant,* one of Malpede's most direct and straightforward plays, but also one which hits the deepest emotional notes. Set in the present, it shows a human and an animal, both, like the characters in *Us*, bearing deep emotional wounds, but who, unlike the characters in *Us*, sense a kindred need for healing through change in the other and grope painfully and determinedly toward it. A bridge between them is created by a migrant child, who bears deep psychic wounds of her own. The apotheosis of change that will free these separated and suffering souls is clearly anticipated but not achieved in this drama. To turn to another classic parallel, *Us* may be seen as bearing parallels to Dante's *Inferno*, a place of continual pain and suffering with no hope of change. *Blue Valiant,* in contrast, has more the feeling of a *Purgatorio* in which suffering has not disappeared, nor happiness been assured, but where the promise of eventual change to a happier and more fulfilled condition is clearly felt.

Two plays in this collection in fact offer a vision of this fulfilled condition, offering at least a glimpse of a *Paradiso* beyond the division and sufferings of the lower worlds. The deceptively simple titles, *Other Than We* and *Better People,* suggest at first an observation based on contrast, between some accepted norm and something else "other" or "better." Hardly surprisingly, their web of reference is much more complex. "Better," for example, bears an ironic double meaning, suggesting both the "better" humans sought by the hubristic scientists and the actual "better" beings of a completely different sort which eventually emerge. The dramatic arcs of these two plays are similar. Both begin in dystopic future worlds, move through a crisis and experience a metamorphosis quite outside the control of the manipulative human agents. The result is a totally new order of being, hopefully free of the divisive and self-destructive features of the old order.

"Quite outside their control" is the key concept here, to which one might add quite outside even their comprehension. The enormity of this change is far greater than anything envisioned by Ovid because the assumption of how the universe operates has itself radically changed. For Ovid, metamorphosis was a dynamic in the hands of the gods alone, not of man. It was the gods, however whimsical and inscrutable, who were thought to determine the course of history and the dynamics of change. With the passing of time, however, humanity essentially banished the gods and seized this power for itself, inaugurating a new era, often referred to as the Anthropocene. The fact that human beings now claimed this power would seem to promise the coming of a world more favorable toward improving the human condition in general. On the contrary, however, humans have proven no better, and arguably much worse at this responsibility than were the Greek gods. The story of Frankenstein's monster haunts the Anthropocene, and human planning has created such horrors as the Holocaust and the atomic bomb. In short, the human ability to change the world has grown steadily both greater and more dangerous.

Better People and *Other Than We* consider this growing danger, if from different perspectives, and ultimately share a common hope. Humanity's unchecked desire to explore and more importantly to control every part of the universe, including humanity itself, could be examined from almost infinite perspectives. Malpede has chosen to represent it in two of its most widely recognized and dangerous aspects. *Other Than We* deals with surely the most familiar example of Anthropocene mismanagement — the massive and largely negative impact of human activity upon the entire ecosystem, from climate change to species extinction. In this drama the world has been irrevocably changed by "The Deluge," a clearly climate-related Anthropocene catastrophe. *Better People* explores the dangers of human intervention in an area less widely reported in the current media, but one of equal consequence to humanity — genetic engineering of the human race itself. Although this play does not begin, like *Other Than We*, after human activity has brought about a major catastrophe, its major characters are already themselves products of grotesque and nightmarish experimentation, one of them created from Jewish sperm collected by the Nazis.

In both plays, however, a new and clearly superior order finally appears, not by the eco-challenging experimentation of the human scientists but almost in spite of it. In both plays it enters the dramatic action through a non-speaking character, a body and form quite outside the established world of the play. In *Better People*, this is the Beast, described by Malpede as a "Yak with Kudu horns, a rare, near extinct species." Even before the mid-play appearance of the Beast, its appearance is anticipated by Edward, the most sympathetic of the scientists, who intuits the word "rendezvous" as the single linguistic tie he has with the Beast. That thin connection seems however to give him an insight into the creative heart of the universe itself — what he calls, in unconscious echo of Ovid, "the ability to generate form." Edward is ultimately unable, however, to use his Anthropocene strategies to allow him to fully reach that heart, even when, later, he is literally swallowed by the Beast. In the phantasmagoric end of the play, though, he moves out of his modern library and through an Ovidian world, becoming a series of animals. At last the Anthropocene laboratory disappears, replaced by the symbol of apotheosis ending each section of Dante's epic — a star-strewn night sky. But this metamorphosis, even apotheosis, still remains in the more familiar universe. Edward and the Beast lie down together, but do not merge. They remain separate entities, and the play ends with the word rendezvous. Two entities have met and made critical contact, but they have not attained the assimilation necessary for a full metamorphosed, Ovid's change, of "forms into new bodies."

It is from this perspective that I see *Other Than We* as both an affirmation and completion of the dynamics of metamorphosis suggested in *Better People*. In the earlier play the walls of the laboratory disappear only at the end, and the ultimate metamorphosis of Edward, if it occurs, is not shown. In *Other than We,* the four protagonists escape from the laboratory (Dome), the authoritarian last outpost of the Anthropocene world, to develop, outside that world, a new post-human form that will hopefully grow into an entity in harmony with itself and the universe. These innovative "forms in new bodies," appropriately called "The Newbies," are still developing at the end of the play and are visible (to our human eyes) as "merely flashes of light." A more central figure involved in this process is the wise elder Opa, who actually completes the change into a new form to which each of these plays, in its own way, seems to aspire. Malpede's stage direction itself calls this a "metamorphosis," and what occurs is not simply the miraculous change of a man into a bird, which bears close visual similarity to many sequences in Ovid. The bird is what our human senses can register, like the flashes of light, but Opa has joined the Newbies in a place beyond human imagination. Perhaps his metamorphosis is better evoked not by the words of Ovid, but by the haunting and visionary words that Shakespeare puts into the mouth of Ariel, who, like the Newbies, is a non- or post-human voice.

> Nothing of him that doth fade
> But doth suffer a sea-change
> Into something rich and strange.

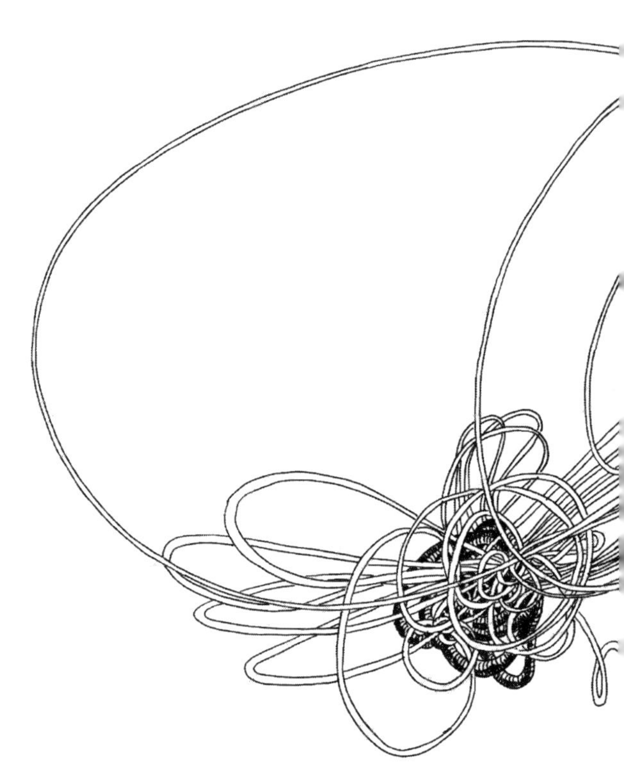

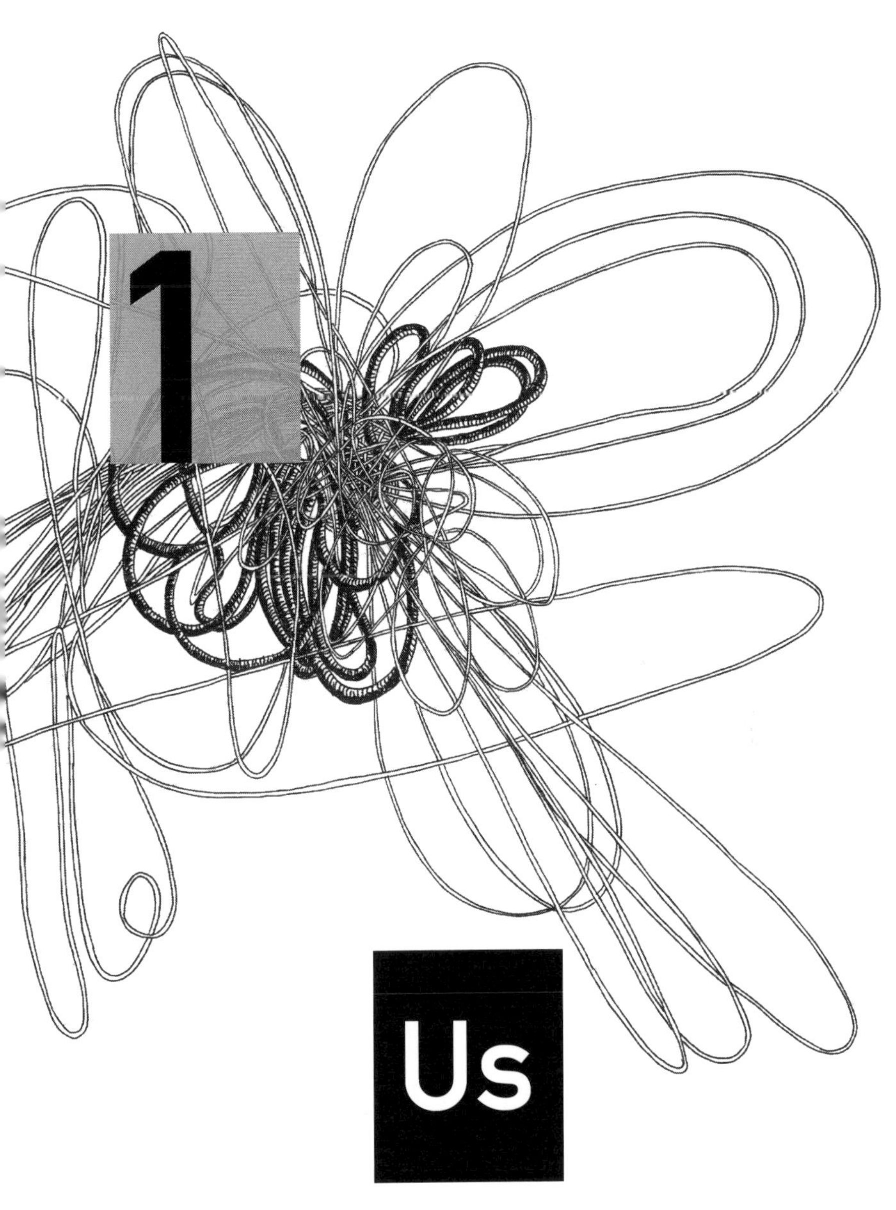

Us

So it is said, "all songs are Holy, the Song of Songs is the Holy of Holies." King Solomon composed three books, two of which, Proverbs and Ecclesiastes, are full of moral sayings and the fear of God, and in them there is much talk of purity and devoutness. But in the Song of Songs such words do not occur. Because of the great power of its holiness, it does not appear to be holy at all. ~ Hasidic Tale

In memory of Julian Beck & Jean Genet

CHARACTERS

This memory play is written to be performed by two actors, who double in the six roles.

TONY, Hannah's father, Italian American

CORA, Hannah's mother, an assimilated American Jew

SYLVIE, Michel's mother, of French extraction, living in Algeria, poor. Later, she marries, lives in France, has money

THE MAN WHO COMES IN THROUGH THE WINDOW, Michel's father, an Algerian

HANNAH, born with the bomb in 1945

MICHEL, child of the French/Algerian War

Time: 1945–1985.

The original set for *Us* was 60 feet long, 18 feet high, and 3 feet wide. Different scenes were located in different parts of this large construction. For instance, Tony's car, in which he seduces his daughter, hung from the ceiling in the far upper right corner of the set. On this huge, narrow set, the actors, as they climbed about, appeared to be constantly in danger. In the original production, the two actors changed wigs and simple costumes as they switched from character to character. The set was designed by Judith Malina, who directed the play's premiere production in 1987; it was realized by Ilion Troya, a member of The Living Theatre, co-founded by Judith Malina and Julian Beck.

SCENE 1

Hannah's sudden recall of life in her parents' house in the United States, the 1950s.

[*Tony throws a female dummy (Cora, his wife) against a wall.*]

TONY. Filthy, fucking, pissing whore, cunt.

[*Bam. The "woman" is bashed against the wall.*]

I ought to spread your legs wide open and piss on you. You're not worth the goddamn money it takes to feed you dinner. Whore. Cunt.

[*He throws "her" against the wall again, and again.*]

Slut. Fucking piss pot. Shit hole. Cunt. Whore. Nothing but a goddamned whore. You only stay with me for my money. Bitch. You're not worth the chair your ass is on. Cunt.

[*He beats the "woman" even as he yells at her. His rage increasing, he molests her every way he can.*]

Dirty Jew. Dirty, fucking, pissing Jew. Jew-girl. Whoring Jewish bitch. Jew-bitch. Fucking Jewish bitch. You're not worth an asshole fuck. Dirty Jewish bitch. Jew-cunt. Filth.

[*Again, the "woman" is slammed against the wall.*]

Sick, uppity bitch. Dirty, stinking, whoring, pissing, sick lady bitch. I ought to stick my prick so far up your cunt you crack in half, like a lobster, cunt. Rotten stink pot. Cunt.

[*The "woman" is thrown against the wall, again.*]

Whore. Rotten, stinking, fat, smelly cunt. I ought to suck the insides out of you. I ought to suck you until there's nothing left. Until you flatten out like a popped balloon. Piss pot. Ugly, stinking, flabby, fat-assed bitch.

[*Bam, the "woman" hits the wall. But this time, the rage is ended. Tony kneels at "Cora's" feet, holds her in his arms. He weeps.*]

Oh, baby, baby, forgive me. Please baby, please. Forgive me, please. I love you, baby, baby. I love you. I do. I'll make it up to you. I will. What do you want? What do you want? Dinner on the town. A red dress, made of silk? Those stockings with rhinestone studded ankles? What, baby, what? A new washer, dish washer? Diaper service? What? I won't hit you again. Oh, God, how could I hit you? How could I hit? How? Baby, baby, I love you. How could I hit you? I love you. Please, baby, please. Oh, yes, yes, yes. You know I do. Yes, help me. Help me. I need you. Please, baby, please. I need you. How could I hit you? I love you. How could I hit you? How?

[*He weeps at "his wife's" feet. Then takes off his hat, or wig. Long hair falls down. He takes off his suit jacket and pants, revealing a woman dressed simply in skirt and top. "He" is his daughter, Hannah. She stands.*]

HANNAH. I was a child in that house. I was a child watching that, hearing those words. I was a child behind closed doors, half asleep in my bed, alone at night, hearing those sounds. What was going on? Hiding behind chairs, choking down food, not hearing what I heard, lost in a book, doing homework, in bed, pillow between my legs, alone in my room for 16 years.

[*She turns on the "woman," her mother, and beats her.*]

HANNAH. Cunt. Whore. Filthy, pissing, fucking, dirty, stinking Jew-girl, whore. Bitch. Cunt.

[*She composes herself.*]

I was born, born of ash. Born of ash borne across the sea, on a hot wind, smelling of death. A wisp of ash, a particle, a flake, infected my mother's womb. No egg. No sperm, but this odd smelling thing. Ash of my ancestors, Abraham,

Sarah, and the rest, beaten as they walked, beaten from the cattle cars, beaten as they choked, choked on prayers. I was born of ash into ash. Born of ash into a world of ash. Destined to become, to be, to reveal myself an insubstantial thing. World of ash which was, which once was hot, fire, hot, fiery flesh.

[*Hannah turns on "her mother," beating her again.*]

Bitch. Bitch. If it wasn't for you, I'd be free. Free. Free, do you hear it, bitch? Free. I'd be free. Healthy and free. Free, baby, free. Do you hear?

[*She rips open the dummy's stomach, pulling out the figure of a baby, herself; now she speaks words her mother might have spoken as she held the baby, Hannah.*]

Oh, baby, baby, forgive me, forgive, forgive me, please. Forgive me, please, baby, please, forgive. Oh, somebody help me, please, someone come to me, please, someone help me, please, oh, please. Take her away. Take her away. Take. Take her. Someone come take her away. Away. Take her away from me. Before I . . .

[*She lifts "the child" high as if to smash her on the ground.*]

Before I. Before . . .

[*She brings the child to her breast.*]

Before I die. Take her away . . . before I . . . take her away. Take. Someone come take her away. Take her away from me. Take.

[*She holds the doll at arm's length, offering her to the audience.*]

SCENE 2

[A middle-class home in France. A beautiful woman sits at a dressing table, her face reflected out toward the audience by a large mirror. She is slightly larger than life. Her face is a realistic, impassive mask. Her heels are very high; her shoulders are padded. Her hair, a wig, is a bright, artificial blond. But she is not grotesque. She is simply large as adults seem very large to young children, and very beautiful, stylish, and somewhat cold in the way that a concern for self-image and style above all make someone cold.]

SYLVIE. Don't tell me that because I don't want to hear it. I don't want to hear it because it is not true. It's not true because it could not possibly have happened. Because it could not possibly have happened it is not true and I don't want to hear it. Do you want to kill me? Do you want me dead? Please, if you want to amuse me tell me something funny. Tell me something funny that happened to you today. Tell me something smart. Something smart that you said or did. You are very smart, you know, very, very smart. Tell me something smart. Tell me something smart that you said. Show me something that you made. Or tell me how I look. Do I look nice to you, tonight? Do I look pretty? To you? How is my hair? Do you like the color? It's a new color, a new tint. Is it too light? Too dark? You are always so observant. Do you like my hair?

[She takes off her wig and throws it on the ground. Now, turns toward the audience.]

Do you like my face? Do you like my face today? I'm wearing a new lipstick, a new shade. I don't often wear such a rosy color, not in winter. In summer, perhaps, but not in winter. In fall? Yes, a rosy color in fall is all right, isn't it? A rosy color to remember by as the leaves drop. Do you like my eyes? It's sweet of you to say so. You like my face. I'm glad. I made it up just for you. It's true. I made my face up just for you. No one else is home, tonight. Who else would I have made my face up for, if not for you?

[*She takes off the mask, revealing a man's face — the Mother has been played by the actor who also plays her son. She does not break character. In fact, it almost seems that as the mask comes off "her" character intensifies, as it might in a dream.*]

Look at my dress, darling. It's nice, isn't it? A little tight. My figure wasn't ruined until the second child. Until you came. You ruined my figure. Ruined it. But never mind, we won't talk about that tonight. I can still get away with a tight dress. Don't you think? It's just you and me. Just us. Help me with the zipper, dear, will you? Help me zip it up.

[*The actor reaches around his back and unzips the dress, stepping out of it. Now he is left with platform heels. Wig, mask, and dress lie on the floor at his feet.*]

These shoes are killing me, really they are. I only wore them because you like them. You're always telling me how much you like these shoes. It's so adorable when you talk about my feet. Everybody thinks so. Really, it's so cute.

[*The actor takes off the shoes and puts them at the foot of the dress. The "mother" lies laid out, so to speak, on the floor, the actor is wearing light pants and a T-shirt, but still does not break character.*]

Now, give me a kiss, dear. Give me a kiss.

[*He kisses the mask.*]

That's a good boy. That's mama's darling boy. That's enough, now, enough. Don't smudge me, please, don't smudge.

[*He puts the mask back on his face.*]

Don't rumple my hair. It took hours to get it right. Yes, dear, that's sweet, but don't rumple my hair, please, be careful, be careful, do you want to ruin my hair? You don't want to ruin my hair. Of course not.

[*He puts the wig back on his head.*]

You're such a handsome boy. You're mama's beauty boy, mama's little pet. You have such a pretty face. Yes, darling, yes. I just have to get out of this dress.

[*The actor puts the dress on.*]

Help me with the zipper, if you can, dear. Be careful. Be careful, don't catch my flesh. Be careful with your mother, careful. You know how much I love you. Be careful what you say.

[*The actor puts the shoes on and seats himself at the dressing table, as at the start.*]

You'll kill me if you talk like that. André is an angel. An angel, do you hear. Your brother did not put his finger up your asshole. He did not masturbate you. He did not make you suck him off until he came. He did not sodomize you, over and over again. He did not make you promise not to tell. He did not hold you down and sodomize you. He did not say he'd kill you if you told. Don't tell me this because I don't want to hear it. I don't want to hear it because it is not true. It is not true because it could not possibly have happened. Because it could not possibly have happened it is not true and I don't want to hear it. Do you want to kill me? Do you want me dead?

[*She swings her perfectly coiffed and made-up self out toward the audience and stares at them.*]

SCENE 3

[The front room of a dilapidated house in a poor workers' quarter of Algiers. Sylvie lives a crowded, uncomfortable life here with her first son, André. She is seen leaning from a window, bathed in the green-white light of a full moon, as the Man jumps in the window opposite.]

SYLVIE. Turn around and go back the way you came. Get out.

MAN. Turn my back on you, Sylvie? You look too beautiful tonight.

SYLVIE. Don't flatter me because I don't want to hear it. Not from you. I don't want to hear it because you'll make me do something I don't want to do.

MAN. I only came to see the kid.

SYLVIE. You came in through the window.

MAN. I came in with the moonlight. There's a full moon tonight.

SYLVIE. So what?

MAN. I saw you learning out the window the first time I passed. That's why I came back. I saw you sucking up that light, like a sea sponge. I saw you glittering in the dark.

SYLVIE. André is asleep.

MAN. Such a fancy French name you've given my son, Sylvie, like your own.

SYLVIE. André is asleep. Now get out.

MAN. Better he shouldn't see me. Better he shouldn't know who I am. With a name like that. I'll just look at him.

SYLVIE. If it was up to you "your son" would be dead.

MAN. That's why I found a good mama for him. I know who I am, the shadow light riding in and out on the dark side of the moon. Dance with me, Sylvie, dance.

SYLVIE. Don't give me those sweet words because I know what those sweet words mean. They're empty, just like you are. Get out. And do me a favor. Use the door.

MAN. Don't be mad at me, Sylvie. You know who I am. I said I loved you. I do. I said I'd come back. Here I am.

SYLVIE. Get out.

MAN. What do you want? A man who comes in every night through the door? A reliable man, who can't see into you? Who reads the paper all night and shakes his head but doesn't understand where he is, what is going on? A "good" man who falls asleep in his chair when he could be smelling you?

SYLVIE. Don't start with the fancy talk.

MAN. Sylvie, I'm the man for you. You know it. You do. You know where we've been. I'm the one who wakes you up. I've set you singing. Singing, Sylvie, with my touch. I've set your flesh to song. Sylvie, I've seen you turn wilder than the night sea, beautiful, so beautiful you take my breath away. If you want what we have, you have to stand a little pain. Dance with me, Sylvie, dance.

[*She walks away from him. He puts a record on the record player.*]

MAN. Hey, love, want a drink?

[*The tango music begins as suddenly, furiously, inescapably, they fuse. The two bodies rush together, compelled by some inner cellular truth. They mate. The man is left, curled at her feet, but even as she speaks, he disappears from her side.*]

SYLVIE. His lavender cock stuck straight out,

washed in the silver moonlight.

Starved, I leapt for that light.

I lapped it up with my thighs,

curled at his side. When I reached out again

he was gone. The empty moon hung in the sky

and I was ocean-drugged, trapped by the swollen tide.

[*His voice comes back to her, as if from a recurrent dream.*]

MAN. Hey, love, want a drink?

SYLVIE. I was walking away. I was walking away when his string snapped me back. I was almost safe. But it's done. Over and done. I'd better not give it another thought. He's gone for good this time and I'll spear the fish he left.

[*She takes a long, difficult drink of abortifacient, spitting the remains out on the floor.*]

SYLVIE. I paid good money for this foul stuff. She better have told me right. Feeling me like that. Clucking her tongue in my face. This better work. It better do more than make me sick. At least he's gone. He hasn't been back. Don't be afraid little one. Go back where you came from. Someone else will take you in. Turn around, now, go. Back over the window sill on that beam of light. Whiskey on his breath. Dark eyes flashing sex.

MAN. [*Again, he speaks as if from a dream.*] You know where we've been.

SYLVIE. Get out. Leave me alone. Prying myself open, open like a can of fish. Wouldn't do it herself. Not for me. I'm French. I told her. I told her who the father is. He's one of yours. She shook her head, afraid I'd turn her in. I begged.

How I begged. She gave me this hook. It better be clean. This better not ruin me. I better come out whole. Like I was. I better come out all right. Now the cramps. Now the cramps and the blood. What a relief it will be. Squatting on the toilet, spitting it out.

Let it hurt. Oh God, let it hurt. Let me go double with pain. But let it end.

MAN. That's how I am. If you want pleasure like we have, you have to stand a little pain.

SYLVIE. I was walking away.

MAN. Hey, love, want a drink?

[*They fuse again.*]

SYLVIE. His lavender cock stuck straight out,

washed in the silver moonlight.

I leapt for that light.

Lapped it up. When I reached out again

he was gone. The empty moon hung in the sky

and I was ocean-drugged, trapped by the swollen tide.

[*This time, it's as if Sylvie is giving birth to the man. She works him out from between her legs. She sits as if she holds the newborn baby-man in her lap. She speaks to the man-child who looks so trustingly at her.*]

SYLVIE. So you don't want to eat. Who are you to turn up your nose? You think I like this any better than you? You're pulling me all out of shape. I can't afford fancy food. You look just like he does. Wouldn't you know. I'm giving you a good French name. I'm calling you Michel. And you better stay out of my way. I've got to find a new man. That's easier said than done with two kids hanging around. So if you don't like the milk, you can starve. Come on, eat. I know how you feel. I could cry, too. Shut up, now, and eat.

[*The child in her arms is Michel. He escapes from her grasp, yelling at his mother.*]

MICHEL. I dream of hands. Hands clawing my eyes. The same dream all my life. Until I stopped dreaming at all. André told me. He told me the secret. He saw. You tried to get rid of me twice. He told me what you did. Things you put inside yourself, trying to hook me like a fish. But nothing you do ever works.

SCENE 4

[*The woman, Cora, Hannah's mother, is in bed. She holds her infant daughter at arm's length. The bed is perpendicular to the floor so that the actors, while leaning against it, are actually fully visible to the audience.*]

CORA. Someone come. Someone come, take her away. Take her away from me. Take.

[*Hannah's father, Tony, enters*]

TONY. Give her to me. Can't you do anything right? She's wet. She's been crying half the night.

[*He takes the child, holds her to his chest, begins to walk, rocking, crooning.*]

All right, *piccolina.* Daddy's little one. Daddy's little love. Hush, Hannah, hush, Daddy's here. Daddy's got you in his arms. Daddy's holding you safe. What do you want? A place in the sun? Music? Do you want music all around? Do you want to dance out under the moon? Dance under the stars in the night? Let Daddy hold you up. He'll pluck down a star for you. The brightest one. You'll sparkle. You'll shine. You'll fly so high. You can have anything, anything at all. You're Daddy's little girl. You can have all the things Daddy never had. Close your eyes, now, dream. Anything you dream of you can have.

CORA. Tony, she's quiet. Come to bed.

TONY. Shut up. She just closed her eyes.

[*Cora rolls over and sleeps.*]

TONY. Daddy's baby, yes. Yes. Dream of sweet things, a pink ruffled dress, teddy bears, a white Cadillac with the top down, long hair blowing in the wind. Daddy's girl, sleep, dream. You can sleep next to Daddy, but not if you cry.

[*He puts the doll-baby in bed on one side of him. He is in the middle of the bed, his wife on his other side.*]

TONY. [*To Cora*] Hey, baby, you awake?

[*She rolls away from him.*]

TONY. [*He turns to the child.*] You woke up? You little skunk. Hush, now, hush. Are you wet? Let me open up your diaper. Just to check. Oh, baby, baby, yes, yes. Once. That's all. Just once. Just once more. Baby, how good you feel. How good. So new, so warm, so wet. Daddy loves you. Yes. Daddy loves his little girl. Hush, now, hush. Go to sleep.

[*He turns to his wife.*]

Cora, wake up. Give me your mouth on my cock.

CORA. Tony, stop.

TONY. Come on. I just got the kid to sleep so we could have some time. Come on, baby, come on.

[*Cora rolls over on top of Tony.*]

Yes, baby, yes. Do me, do me, baby. Oh, baby, so good, so good. You do me so good. Yes. Yes.

[*Tony runs his hands through her hair, pushing her head down between his legs.*]

CORA. Tony, what have you done? The child's in bed. Tony, what have you done, the child's in bed with us.

TONY. Shut up. She's asleep. What does she know? She's a baby. Shut up. Open your legs. Come on, baby, come on. I need you. You know I do. I need you. I need you, baby, please. I need you.

[*He rolls on top of her.*]

TONY. You're so good, baby, so sweet.

[*He rolls off of Cora and on top of the infant-doll at his other side.*]

TONY. Oh, baby, baby, yes, yes, open up, open up, just once, open up, now, once, open up. Yes. Yes. Just once. Just once more.

[*He rolls back off of her.*]

CORA. What have you done, Tony, what? The child is in bed with us. Tony, what have you done?

TONY. Shut up. She's asleep. She's a baby. What does she know. Open your legs. Come on, baby, come on. I need you. You know I do. Please, baby, please.

[*He rolls back on top of Cora.*]

You're so good, so good, baby, so good.

[*He rolls back on top of the doll.*]

Oh, baby, baby, yes, once, just one time, open up, just once, open up, now, yes, yes.

[*He rolls off of the doll.*]

CORA. Tony, what have you done? The child's in the bed. Tony, what have you done? The child's in bed with us.

TONY. Shut up. She's asleep. What does she know. She's a baby. What does she know. Open your legs. Come on, baby, be good to me, now. You're the best, baby, the best I ever had.

[*Tony buries his head in Cora's lap.*]

CORA. Oh, Tony, what have you done?

[*She reaches for the infant-doll, picks her up, holding her at arm's length, the man's head buried in her lap.*]

She's the only one you never hit. She's the only one you ever loved.

SCENE 5

[Michel outside the house in Algiers, 1956. He is eleven years old. Sylvie at her dressing table inside.]

MICHEL. We were leaving Algiers. She was going to take me away. I saw a man whistling at the window. Whistling at the window. Calling someone. Whistling a song. Then he was gone. Quick, through the backyard. Over the fence. Looking this way and that. I ran. I ran after that song.

[Unseen by Sylvie, Michel listens to her as, roaming the house, she begins to pack her things.]

SYLVIE. That bastard came back again. Whistling at the window, like he's calling a dog. "I'm going out with Claude," I told him right to his face. "Claude is hard working, smart. Claude is steady. He comes home every night. If we get out of this country alive, if we get out of this war, if we get to France before we are killed, Claude will be a success." How he hated that. How he grew stony with rage. I laughed. I laughed in his face. Claude has a mechanical mind. Engineer, accountant, Claude could be anything. Money in our pockets. A private bedroom. I could open a shop. I'm marrying Claude. I told him that. Claude doesn't like Michel. He gets along with André, but he doesn't like Michel. Michel shakes when Claude is around. He stutters. He makes funny sounds, like motors, like guns. Claude can't stand that. Michel is stupid he says. Says he's trouble, like the other one. I'm lucky Claude will have me with two sons. Lucky he'll take me away. But he doesn't like Michel.

MICHEL. [*To Sylvie*] He came back. I know he did. He came back for me. He doesn't care about you. He came back for me. I know he did. I don't want to go with you and Claude. I want to stay here with him.

SYLVIE. How can you talk like that? How can you say those things? After all I've done? How can you threaten me? You'll be dead in the street. You'll be killed by one of their bombs. You stay away. You stay away from his kind. Claude is your father now. Claude will take care of you. The other one doesn't care if you're dead or alive. Say it. Say it for me. Call Claude "Papa." Go ahead. Make me proud. Say it for me. I love you so. Call Claude "Papa." That's my special boy. That's my Michel. Claude is your papa now.

[*Transition within the scene to Tony's house. He sits at the kitchen table. Underneath, in the basement, Cora is visible, camped out. She is frying an egg on a hot plate.*]

TONY. She doesn't love me. Never did. Married me because of the war. Whore. Neighbors saw them. They climbed into the window in broad day. Neighbors said, "Your wife. Your wife and the actor who was in that play." Climbed through the window of the empty house. In the middle of the day. She is the most beautiful woman I ever saw. Smart, too. Knows how to talk. How to talk sweet all right. Doesn't love me, never did. Married me because of the war. Thought I'd be rich. I'm rich all right. I'm killing myself for her and the kid. Jewish bitch. Her kind are all alike. "He was nice to me, Tony." Nice! Haven't I been nice. Haven't I tried. Look at this house. Closet full of clothes. Cleaning woman once a week. Beauty shop. I pulled at her hair. Pulled out a clump of her hair. "In the old country, you'd be dead." Bitch. "If you leave me, I'll take the kid. You'll starve if you leave me." Don't leave me, Cora, don't leave me. Can't you love me, if you try? "What kind of mother fucks around. You'll never see your kid again." Can't you love me? She doesn't answer anymore. Sleeps in the basement on a cot. Like she's hiding out.

Cora, get the hell upstairs. I got to get to work. I got to eat.

CORA. *[From the basement. Meek, always meek when she speaks to Tony]* Toast is in the toaster, Tony. Pop it down. Orange juice in a covered glass in the fridge. Hot coffee in the pot.

TONY. Get the hell upstairs. I want eggs.

CORA. Eggs are on the stove. In a pan with a lid. The way you like them, Tony, scrambled hard.

[He looks around the kitchen for a moment, confused. Then slams down the stairs, going to work. He returns.]

TONY. Getthehellupstairs. I'm home from work.

CORA. Dinner's on the table. Chicken. Potatoes. Peas. Key lime pie in the fridge.

TONY. Where's the kid?

CORA. I don't know where she is.

TONY. Whadaya mean, you don't know? She's eleven years old. Whadaya mean, you don't know? Get your ass up here.

[Tony storms down the stairs again, to look for Hannah. He comes back.]

Cora, kid's at the neighbors. For Chrissake, come up from the basement. I want sex.

CORA. It's my time of month. I'm going to sleep.

[In the basement, Cora lies down. Tony goes toward the bedroom. Morning comes and he comes back into the kitchen.]

TONY. Get yourself up here. I need food.

CORA. Ironed shirts in the drawer. Breakfast on the table. Cut the banana into the cereal. Hannah's skirt hemmed. Her lunch in the paper bag. Coffee, strong, in the pot.

TONY. All right. Stay in the cellar. Stay there forever.

[Again, he is down the stairs to work. He returns at night.]

TONY. I don't care. Goddamned whore. Goddamned cunt. I'm going out. I got girls. I got girls. Girls at the office. Plenty of girls, I got.

CORA. Spaghetti and sausage in the pot. Bread warming up. Wine glass set out.

[*Tony sits, contemplating his situation. In a few moments, he has an idea. He calls excitedly to his daughter in her bedroom.*]

TONY. Hannah, baby, put your book down. You can't read all night. Hannah, baby, let's go to a show. Come on baby, get your coat. Put your coat on. It's raining, baby. It's raining hard. Come on, Hannah, button up. Let's go, you and me. Let's go to a show. Come on, Hannah, let's go. It's raining hard. Watch out for that puddle there. Follow me. Come on baby, get into the car.

[*They arrive at the car. Tony helps Hannah in. Gets in beside her, starts the motor, off they go.*]

HANNAH. Daddy, go slow. You're driving so fast. Daddy, Daddy, I'm scared. Daddy, listen to me. In school today, we had to hide. Hide in the basement, in the hall, under the big pipes, the pipes wrapped in tape, under the bandaged pipes. Hands over our heads, hiding out. Do you think the Russians will drop the bombs? Daddy, do you think so? Will I live to be old like you?

TONY. Hannah, baby, let's stop the car. Let's stop the car on the side of the road. Don't be frightened, baby, don't be scared. Daddy will hold you in his arms. Once, baby, just one time, let me kiss you on the mouth. Let me kiss you, yes, yes. You love me, baby. I know you do. Daddy doesn't leave you. You know that. Daddy will keep you safe. Daddy doesn't let you down. Daddy's here for you all the time.

[*Tony slowly runs his hand down Hannah's body, from her neck, between her two breasts, to her crotch. Silent and terrified, Hannah stares straight ahead.*]

SCENE 6

[Hannah, at the back door of the house. She is pulled inside by Tony. She resists him. They argue.]

HANNAH. We were watching TV. We were sitting in the TV room watching the late show.

TONY. Get your ass inside this house. What do you mean showing your face here at 3 am? You should sleep in the street. You're just like your mother. A whore. Just like her.

[She pulls away from him.]

HANNAH. I'll sleep in the street. I'll never put foot inside this rotten house.

TONY. Get your ass inside this house. Don't you talk back.

[He grabs her, raising his hand, as if to strike.]

I'll kill that fucking bastard. I'll kill him before . . . You stay away from that bum. I'll kill him if you go near him again. I swear.

HANNAH. We were watching TV . . .

[Now he is all remorse and gentleness.]

TONY. Oh, baby, babe . . . be careful of yourself. You got to do that. I got no time left.

[She is cradled in his arms.]

HANNAH. Daddy, please . . . I . . .

TONY. Baby, help me, I'm scared. I'm sick, baby. Don't make it worse.

HANNAH. Daddy, please, I'm frightened, Daddy, please.

[Her childish need makes him pull away. He begins to search the house for Cora. Hannah trails behind him.]

TONY. Cora! Cora! Help me, Cora, help. I heard what the doctor said. I'm dying. Cora, I got no hope. You got to help me, now.

HANNAH. [*Runs after him*] Daddy, wait. We were watching TV. That's all. Daddy, please, forgive me, Daddy, forgive . . .

TONY. Cora, I'll make it up to you. I'll make it up, all of it, all. We'll be happy, now. Cora, Cora, we got to be happy now. Doctor says there's no time left.

[*He stops, for a moment. Hannah rushes to him.*]

TONY. Baby, baby, baby . . . love . . .

[*He caresses her. Then pushes her away and begins to search for Cora again.*]

TONY. Cora, help me. I'm so scared. I'm scared. Cora, I'm scared. Cora, you're smart. You know how to behave. I love you, Cora. You know that. You're the only one I ever loved.

[*Hannah follows him, but he pays no attention. All his focus is upon Cora, represented by the stuffed dummy who was battered in Scene 1.*]

TONY. You've got to help me, Cora. You're all I have. My own mother, she said, "It's all up for you, Tony. You're finished, you know that." She talked like I was already dead. "You got cancer, Tony, because you married out of your religion." You heard her say that, that's what she said.

Cora, what do you want? A diamond ring? A new car? Wall to wall carpet everywhere, a marble sink? What? What do you want while I can still do for you? Come on, Cora, let's go to the mall. I can still get around.

Cora, you're the only one for me. Yes, Cora, yes. Take me like you used to do. Talk to the doctor for me. Tell him to give us some time. Tell him we'll pay him anything. Stay with me, now, stay with me. Cora, stay. Read to me, Cora, read. Cora, sing to me, baby, sing. We'll be happy, now. We got to be happy now. You'll stay with me, now, stay with me, now, stay with me until I die.

[He is dead on the floor at "Cora's" feet. Hannah puts a black veil over "Cora's" face, and then puts a longer veil on herself.]

HANNAH. I wanted to look beautiful at your funeral. Wanted to look more beautiful than she did. Wanted to look like your bride. I wanted to look like I belonged to you, was yours, I wanted to look like you. "Little Tony," they used to call me that. I wanted to look beautiful, pure. I wanted to look like a virgin bride. Dressed in black, following behind you, following behind, following behind you to the grave. I wanted to look radiant, wild. I wanted to throw myself into the grave. I wanted to look like I belonged to you, was yours, was you, was yours following behind you, following you. People whispered, they did, "oh, how lovely." "How lovely she looks." I wanted to be perfect. Radiant. On that day of days, day I followed you to the grave. Eyes, your eyes. Your eyes staring back from the mirror. I wanted you to see me. I wanted you to see me. I wanted you to see. I wanted you to know me, to know, to know me, to want me, to want, to want me to live. I felt, but I couldn't say how I felt. I felt you were jealous of me dating boys. You died because I grew up. You died and left me alone. You were jealous and you died. I wanted to be your bride. Dressed in black, following behind you, following behind you, following you back. I wanted to throw myself after you into the grave, I wanted to be, to be lost with you, like you, yours. I wanted to keep you, to keep you with me. I wanted you back.

SCENE 7

[*As Michel speaks, warm water showers over him.*]

MICHEL. On long, hot days, I went with my grandmother to the sulfur spring hidden in the hills, the spring where the Arab women bathed. I was a child to them, a skinny French child, ignored in their sovereign world. I swam in the hot, blue sulfur sea between the fat thighs of Arab women, heavy dresses pulled up, bright fabrics turned dark in the sulfur sweat, floating like lilies on the silken ledge, trunk legs planted in mud. Sharp talk drops hit overhead, fragments of family affairs, money exchanged, illnesses, marriages, births, broken now and again by a hot lava laugh flowing from an open throat, primeval flow from beneath the hot sea where I swim in and out of the folds of their flesh. They lift their skirts higher, plant flat feet deeper in the wet mud. I skitter between lush folds of fat. The harsh talk, talk, talk falls on the surface glass overhead.

Two full thighs close over me, squeezing me, wriggling helpless with delight. Flesh walls open above my skinny back, salt from the sea and salt. Seaweed hair and labia lips fall over me. Dizzy on the rhythm of blood rushing to the spot, the heart, the heart loud as a shot. I explode in the silver sea, filling it with fish sperming their way out. Mated with the wet underworld, spent and devoured. Quick, I slap tail-legs against the vice in which I am caught. I spurt up, I arrive, gulping air, born to two faceless breasts. Her hands slap me away with a blow that sets my water lungs hacking. "Nuisance," she yells, "nuisance," slapping at me like a fly. Bellowing out words, she is an elephant mare, standing calm. I dive down. Underneath, she convulses, writhes, glories in the lost underworld where pleasure survives. "Nuisance," she slaps and I dive, laughing between her fat legs. I set my sperm loose in the sulfur sea. For years afterwards, I look hard at the faces of fish, hoping to see my eyes or my mouth, a new creature spawned from those hot afternoons, alive in the hot sulfur sea.

HANNAH. I come to the stable late in the thick autumn dusk. Not used to the cotton pad between my legs or the hot blood collecting, I am walking clumsy, I think. I want to find others who smell as I smell, others who know the ragged edges of the flesh. I breathe in the horses, their deep dull eyes and their sweat, their golden urine mixed with the straw at their feet, and the sweet smell of decay rising between my legs. I am wrapped in this mist, grabbed, taken under the earth, like a root, determined and wet.

Cigarette smoke, stale and sharp, the hard laughs of the men exploding like bombs. Their muscular arms laced with blue veins hang on the rail of the ring while a dark stallion they've loosened seizes a mare between his forelegs and mounts her. They are yelling at him, laughing, urging him on. I put my hands to my ears. "Fuck the bitch. Fuck her." The two creatures crazed with desire abandon their shapes, becoming liquid and fire. I watch white light rise from the steam of their fusing. But I cannot block out the men's words, or their laughing. A clot of hot blood falls from me onto the thick cotton pad. Shame sends a hot current through me. Stallion and mare stand apart, heads hanging low. The men leave them there, turn, satisfied and go. There is no sound but our animal breathing. I enter the ring. The mare is quiet, pulled into herself, lost. I am drawn to the stallion. How did I not see he's been wounded. His long stalk utterly exposed. His soul spring reddened, wrinkled, sucked at and emptied. I want to kneel at his feet in the sawdust. I want to take his wound into my mouth, wrap my lips around his hurt flesh. I want to hold him there gently, while he gathers himself, while he mends. I lay my cheek against his wet neck, making low soothing sounds. I lead him into the barn. Slip a hard metal bit into the warm wet folds of his mouth.

[*Hannah bridles Michel, who kneels and takes the bit, then she lays herself against his back.*]

Let's go, now, I whisper. We move out into the night. I give him his head, lay myself low on his back. Together we run through the deep autumn woods, leaves breaking under our weight, moon lighting our path, moon drenching us in white light. I sing into his ears because he cannot, because he runs for me as I sing.

SCENE 8

[Michel ties Hannah's hands above her head with the reins of the bridle. He holds her bound as he speaks.]

MICHEL. My grandmother tied rabbits to the spigot in the tin sink. She picked up a knife. With one stroke sliced them open, from chest to crotch.

[He demonstrates on her body.]

Their guts spilled out, long intestinal ropes, liver, kidneys, heart, singing against the tin sink. We come from the ocean, you know, our blood is the same as the hot sea water. Why, then, do we hold ourselves apart?

[He drops her hands.]

HANNAH. My grandmother had chicken breasts delivered in cardboard boxes with the groceries. She cooked them for hours in their own fat in the high tin pot. During World War II, she ate chicken with her fair-haired German-Jew in-laws in Palm Beach restaurants beneath signs that said, "No Jews Allowed." What strong stomachs we human beings have.

MICHEL. I was coming around the corner, carrying the rabbit in the cloth sack. Waiting for the blood to spatter against my grandmother's big breasts, when I heard the animal cry. When I saw a man's guts spill against the hot stones, while he watched animal-like. I saw him go down on his knees. I saw him shovel his guts back into his belly with his hands. I watched while he held his wet self in his arms.

[Hannah goes down on her knees. She keeps trying to shovel her guts back into her stomach as she cries.]

HANNAH. I don't know their names.

I am not a part of their group.

I don't know.

I don't know anything.

I never saw them before.

I'm dying. Oh, my God, I'm dying.

[*She speaks these works as a litany underneath the beginning of Michel's speech.*]

MICHEL. People were blown up in movie theaters, or cafes, churches, or stores, on the streets, in their beds at home. Was it the Algerian Fellaghas or the French soldiers? Freedom fighters or mercenaries? You could never tell. Who were they? What had they done? What crime? Were they fighting for the people? Had they betrayed their own? Who did they leave? Who did they leave behind? That man, holding his guts in his hands, was that man my father? My father? Freedom fighter, night crawler, coward, jerk. In the resistance, the army, the police, plain clothes cop, terrorist chief, truck driver, liar, informer, waiter at the cafe where they met, did he know much, did he pass bombs? Once, I saw a hand, just a hand, lying in the gutter. Did that hand touch my mother? "Go on, get out, leave me alone." The head I saw on the fence post, did that head talk? "I only came to see my son." I pieced him together a hundred times from a hundred different parts. How I wanted to know, to know him, to know him, knowing me. How I searched, searched everywhere. The head of a doctor, the guts of a waiter, the heart of a worker, the long, thin, beautiful woman-like hand in the gutter so like my own. The legs of a farmer, the nuts and prick of a student, the eyes of a fighter, gouged out and left for the flies. The slippery noise of blood flooding the throat and the lungs, my father's song to his son.

[*He is on top of Hannah, her legs wrapped around him.*]

One night, during an air raid, I made love for the first time. My aunt wrapped me between her strong legs. I made silent love on the cold floor, while the bombs exploded over our heads. I made noiseless love, careful not to move, careful not to move too much, careful not to bump my grandmother or anyone else who lay on the crowded floor, stiff and still. I felt myself swell while the bombs fell and I thought I would come apart in her arms, while she laughed her wild laugh in my ear.

[*Settled in Hannah's arms, he speaks to her.*]

So you see, Hannah, why in the refugee camp when I was 11, I went immediately to the Red Cross tent and volunteered. I carried water to the wounded and told myself, when I grow up, I will become a healer.

And do you also understand, Hannah, why it is I cannot attach myself to anyone?

SCENE 9

[*The actors never touch. However, this is the erotic ballet.*]

HANNAH. It's not a casual affair. Not to me, it's not. I've had them. It's not a casual affair.

MICHEL. I want only a casual affair. I want only someone to fuck. I need a little emotional diversion. I need some new emotional life.

HANNAH. Good morning, my love. I love you.

MICHEL. I found your note on my pillow. You are an exquisite lover, Hannah. We are having a great time.

HANNAH. When I look at you, I want to lick you all over. Your asshole tastes sweet to me.

MICHEL. The things you say. The things you cry in the night. "Take me. Take me." Yes, I will take you. I will take you as long as you want. But, you frighten me with your talk.

HANNAH. Don't fear, dear one. It will be over soon. Soon enough. Over and done. The flesh will stop straining to become. The two-throated pipe will break on the song.

MICHEL. Hannah, can you come to me, now? Can you fly? I dreamt of you all night. I woke with such longing in my flesh. I woke feverish, in sweat. I woke with you in my blood.

HANNAH. Oh, my sweet, sweet one. You make love like a woman. Like a woman you lean into me. Like a woman, you moan in my arms, you give me your milk, rise and fall. In what silver sea, wrapped in what goddess's laugh, were you spawned? What blessing gave you to me?

MICHEL. Hannah, you are erotic everywhere. The hair on

your ass, that soft, soft hair. Your feet, your toes, your toes kneading my balls.

HANNAH. How did you become so fierce and so gentle?

MICHEL. Will you catch my balls in your mouth? Will you swallow my balls?

HANNAH. Yes, of course, I will swallow them whole. I will sprout each seed you hoard in your moist lavender sacks. I will drop a new race from between your legs. I will make you Abraham.

MICHEL. Your smell. I cannot get your smell off my hands. I shower. I wash. My skin smells of you, Hannah, all the time. I walk in your aura, your light, as if I were of you, formed by you, made, molded inside, pushed out bearing your taste.

HANNAH. I write in the morning, in the morning, with my legs apart. I feel like I'm straddling a field, straddling the land, smelling the growing, smelling the growing of the grain. I breathe you in, breathe out an image, a thought. Effortless because the body already knows. In the beginning was the word. No. In the beginning was this rich scent. This lost memory of love.

MICHEL. I was so deep into you, from two sides, my cock and my hand almost met, but for a silk curtain of flesh. I wanted to draw the veil aside.

HANNAH. I am found. For the first time, I am seen.

MICHEL. I like to take you out of your mind. I work hard to free you from words, to set you free of yourself, free of us, free of me.

HANNAH. The taste. The taste of a man. As if I ate something unformed. As if I ate newborn flesh. As if I ate life.

MICHEL. I want to put my head inside you. I want to crawl into you. To be lost, spinning in space, the holiness dropping, dropping to earth in the dark.

HANNAH. Only let me lick you again. Before you become my own inside, let me taste. Before you vanish from my sight, leave your sweet taste in my mouth.

MICHEL. Why is it perfect with us, Hannah? Why is it better than it has ever been?

HANNAH. Nothing we do sullies us, why is that?

MICHEL. Hannah, I go so deep inside you, I forget how to breathe. I am a fish underwater, searching your sea. I want to open you like a lobster. I want to crack you apart. I want to take a child out of you. I want to reach inside and pull a child out. I want to feel my fingers reaching, searching through mud, catching hold, catching hold of the first head, bringing up the first light, bearing the first sight. Hannah, I want life.

HANNAH. Look, look at your lavender cock, draped with my blood. A coat of many colors alive in the sun. Give me your cock. Put your cock in my mouth. I want to suck you dry. Suck you until I am full. Suck you until you melt on my tongue, in my mouth. Give me your wound, your hurt, your broken part. I want to suck you until you grow straight, suck you until I can hear you touching my voice.

[*Now they begin to speak in the other's voice. So that Michel says words that seem to issue from Hannah's experience of their love and Hannah speaks from knowledge of Michel's experience. Feeling with one another in this way, they are truly joined.*]

MICHEL. I want to make you sing. I want to give you my song. To put my song on your tongue, my taste, frothing sea foam. I want to put the sea's song in your flesh. I want to give you the sound: the birth-cry, the lament, the uttering up, the belly-full shout.

HANNAH. I want to take you out of your mind, to feel you spinning as I reach into you. I felt you swirl overhead. I felt you in flight. Did you touch? Did you touch light?

MICHEL. I felt myself splayed apart, cut, like the sacrificed doe dripping blood. Did you taste? Did you taste God when you ate?

HANNAH. Nothing we do sullies us. Why is that?

MICHEL. I want you inside. I want all of you. I want to give birth, to give birth to you. I want to birth you whole, whole and unhurt and alive.

HANNAH. You put such peace into me when we touch. Such peace when I rest in your flesh, when you leak your life into mine.

MICHEL. Are you here with me? Are you here?

HANNAH. Yes, I am here. I am here with you. It is all right. I am here.

MICHEL. Let me go where you lead. Let me open up. I will go. I will leap. I will be the corridor, the tunnel, the channel, the way. I will bring the blessing to earth. I will set it to root.

HANNAH. Yes, my one, yes. Bring me the light on your brow. The first sight. The smells the mother casts over the child. Oneness. The oneness of God.

[*They become themselves again.*]

HANNAH. Were you there with me? Were you there?

MICHEL. Yes, of course. I was there. We are twins. Placenta wrapped. Wet spots on the dark. Don't make me surface, Hannah. Don't beach me. I die in the air, on the land. I die out of the sea.

HANNAH. Put your head inside me again, sweet, sweet prehistoric fish.

SCENE 10

[*The lovers wake.*]

MICHEL. How well we sleep together, Hannah. Without moving. Without moving once.

HANNAH. Where have you been while the flesh slept?

MICHEL. No, Hannah, I do not dream.

HANNAH. When you sleep you seem so utterly gone.

MICHEL. When I sleep, I am gone, Hannah, it's true. I cannot be for you all of the time.

HANNAH. I lie waking next to your skin. I lie tasting the moment you will come back. I cannot bear exile myself in a dream.

MICHEL. When I have a dream, Hannah, I will tell you. When I dream, I will do what the dream tells me to.

HANNAH. I must go . . . I have work . . .

MICHEL. Stay the morning with me.

HANNAH. I need . . .

MICHEL. I know what you need.

HANNAH. I need my work. I need myself back.

MICHEL. Hannah, I've read your book. It is not yet near what you will be. What you have inside. Stay the morning with me.

HANNAH. I need.

MICHEL. I know what you need.

HANNAH. I need your cock, your lavender cock, like a breast, lain in my mouth.

MICHEL. Yes, Hannah, of course.

HANNAH. No. I must dress.

MICHEL. Whatever you wish.

[*They dress as they speak, and, once dressed, they begin to move away from each other as they continue their debate.*]

HANNAH. You will leave me, Michel; you will go.

MICHEL. No, Hannah, I never leave anyone. I come back. I come back when I can.

HANNAH. Marry me, Michel.

MICHEL. If I said, "yes?"

HANNAH. I would run.

MICHEL. I am not constant, Hannah. I am not what you want.

HANNAH. Marry me, Michel.

MICHEL. You know the answer to that.

HANNAH. No, I don't.

MICHEL. If we are together all of the time, we will kill what we have.

HANNAH. No we won't.

MICHEL. I know how it is with passion like ours.

HANNAH. It will grow into something else.

MICHEL. It will die.

HANNAH. Michel, I am hurting this way.

MICHEL. But, Hannah, what can we do?

HANNAH. Work it out. Try.

MICHEL. Why do you always want more, my little Jew? Why do you like to suffer so?

HANNAH. How can we feel what we do and not want . . .

MICHEL. Can you make more money, Hannah? Can you give less time to your work? Can you help me in the office, Hannah? Can you send me to school, if that's what I have to do for myself?

HANNAH. I don't want to take care of you.

MICHEL. Why can't you be happy, now? You have a lover who loves you a lot.

HANNAH. This is hurting, Michel.

MICHEL. If it hurts, you must like it that way. See how your breathing is pinched from sitting all day over your books.

HANNAH. You disgust me, Michel.

MICHEL. Hannah, if you want to rage at how bad your life is, go out on the street, gather your bags full of garbage, and sit, wailing into the gutter. Don't bother me with these words.

HANNAH. All right. We are having a love affair. That's all it is. We will watch it fizzle out. But why do we need it so much? Why is it like air in our lungs?

MICHEL. Hannah, think how lucky you are to have this.

HANNAH. With you.

MICHEL. With anyone.

HANNAH. With you.

MICHEL. With anyone.

HANNAH. Only you exist for me, Michel.

MICHEL. Then take what is here. Don't ask for what we can't have in this life. Hannah, stay the morning with me.

[*He begins to come toward her.*]

HANNAH. I have work to do.

MICHEL. Your work is this pleasure we have. Take it in.

HANNAH. I must go.

MICHEL. Hannah, you give me such joy. You put such peace into my flesh. Can't you be happy, now, with what you have?

[*She comes back toward him, now.*]

HANNAH. If you touch me like that . . .

MICHEL. Yes, Hannah. Leave your suffering behind.

HANNAH. You were so deep inside me.

MICHEL. My cock and my hand almost met. I wanted to draw the veil aside.

HANNAH. I wanted you to kill me, then.

MICHEL. No, Hannah, not this time.

HANNAH. When?

MICHEL. You want me to kill you, Hannah? But, of course, I have already killed you in another life. At an oasis, perhaps.

HANNAH. With a small silver knife.

MICHEL. Before they stoned us to death.

HANNAH. You traced your mark on my womb.

MICHEL. I cut you then myself.

The Arab and the Jew.

Adulterer. Sodomite.

Before they stoned us to death.

The hot sand swallowed our blood.

HANNAH. I knew perfect trust.

I wanted you to kill me, then,

while I was death-blessed.

MICHEL. Hannah, let me take you again from behind.

HANNAH. Take me however you wish. I leave my flesh in your arms.

[*They speak the next speeches simultaneously, aria-like.*]

MICHEL. Let me take you. Let me take you, now. Yes, yes. Are you all right? Then shout, Hannah, shout. Shout as loud as you want.

Someone might come. Someone might. I watch you here on this ledge, this hard, white ledge where I squat, out of sight, watch you writhe, watch you squirm, watch you dance, dance in the palm of my hand. I want to be stretched on that wrack, to be pulled apart, too, be looked at, looked up, looked into, seen. Seen in the hollow spot. The rotting part seen. The stench taken in. What I want most of all as I hang here, spread, spread apart, pulled at and stretched, played with and left, is not to be shamed. I want to feel no shame. Stroked, dirtied, and cleaned, smelled, powdered, and washed. Shameless. Unashamed. Without shame. Without shame in your arms.

HANNAH. Yes. Michel. Yes. Take me. Take me however you wish. I leave my flesh in your arms.

I am lost in a body pile, stinking with shit that slips out after the breathing has stopped. Stinking Jew in a world of Jews, everyone marked, poisons seeping into each womb. Body piles, pits, the whole earth a pit for the dead who lie shitting their prayer: Hear, oh, hear. I crawl, crawling up. Then I know. Then I see. It is a soul pile in which I swim. In the midst of the flesh, rotten and wet, molding like bread, bright souls are piled in a heap. Humming, humming their song. Souls ripe like round apples. Luminous, proud. I reach out. Reach, with my mouth, with my tongue. Irresistible, sweet, soul fruit left by the dead fills me up. I am found. I am fed. Light spreads through my flesh, through

Open and seen. Seen into. Held. Wanted. Wanted like this. As I am. I want to be whole, to be held. I want to heal. Hands reaching. Clawing at me. Don't. Don't make me feel. Don't. I land on the hot stones. Spilled open, crawling toward you. Begging. Don't. Don't hurt me again. Don't let me feel. Don't. Don't.

Love, oh my love, don't cry. Don't cry in my arms. Don't. Am I hurting you? Why do you cry, Hannah, why?

my hollow self. Bright soul light. I am found. I am seen. Ash drops to the ground, like an old skin that I shed. While I cling, cling to the soul pile in which I sing. I am found. I am seen. Made whole on the ripe soul song. The sudden vibrating tone. The slow sound spreading. Everywhere spreading. Light seeping in, spreading through everything. Light giving light. Light drenching me in white light.

Yes, yes. Yes, I am crying. I don't know why I cry. Stop, Michel, stop. You are hurting me, now. Hold me, hold me. Hush, hush. Hold me gentle and close.

MICHEL. Are you here, Hannah? Are you back? Hannah, I like to take you out of your mind. But I want you back with me, now.

HANNAH. You reach so far inside me. You reach so far inside. You touch me where I have not been touched before. What is it with us, what? Why is it like this with us? Why is that?

MICHEL. Take what we have. Take.

HANNAH. It is a mystery.

MICHEL. Do not question it.

SCENE 11

[*Hannah and Michel in bed, asleep; he wakes, waking her.*]

MICHEL. Hannah, wake. I dreamt last night. I was led by a monk in a black robe along the ridge of the mountain range that runs across the top of the world.

"Am I dead?" I asked him. "Follow me," he said. "Have I died?" He led me across the mountain range. I could see the whole world from where we stood. He led me to the place where the water wells up from the earth and flows down the mountain from two sides, filling the oceans of the world. He waved his hand. "Look." I looked around. I saw everything. The whole world spread itself under my feet. And the water ran down. It bubbled and sang. The monk asked for my hand. I laid it down in his own. He drew a knife from his cloak. In one stroke, he punctured my palm. He squeezed the wound. Clots of my blood dropped into all the waters of the world. I saw the water turn red. "Will I be a healer?" "Will I heal or pollute?" I cried out to him. He didn't answer when I spoke. He was gone. I stood there alone. I watched my blood flow. Watched the water turn red as it spilled two ways down the mountain side, spilled into oceans, rivers, and lakes. Red blood from my hand, turning the waters red.

Hannah, do you understand? I must become like a monk. Shut the doors to my cell. I must give myself over to my work. I must study. I need to know more.

HANNAH. Michel, you remembered your dream. You found your dream life. And the dream is new.

MICHEL. It is because of you, Hannah, because of this, because of you filling me up. I used to say, "I have no brain." Remember, Hannah, how I spoke? "I have no brain. I have only the skin on my face, good for fucking and smoking dope." But, now, Hannah, I will work.

HANNAH. I love you, Michel.

MICHEL. Yes, Hannah, I know that you do. But I need energy, now. I need energy for my work. I need support. I need to be left by myself. I need money. Hannah, can you make more money, do you think? Give less time to your work? I'm going to go back to school. I'm going to get my MD. I'm going to be respected, Hannah. I won't be outside anymore. I need someone to help me through school. I need someone to give me support. I'm going back to my wife. She will let me have a mistress. Hannah, you would never do that.

HANNAH. Back to your cow. Something to milk everyday.

MICHEL. Hannah, don't talk like that. I need you in my life. You give me something I don't get. I don't find such passion with anyone else. You give me such peace. You put such peace in my flesh.

HANNAH. No, Michel, no. The feelings will start.

MICHEL. Don't talk. Let me be gentle, now. Once more. Let me lick you everywhere.

[*A transition within the scene occurs as the following scene between Sylvie and Michel's father suddenly surfaces within Michel's unconscious. He is dragged back into the trap of his past.*]

SYLVIE. Once more. One more time. No one will know. Next week, we'll be in France.

MAN. See how good I am. How careful with you. How I need you, my fancy French girl.

SYLVIE. Hush up, your sons are in the next room. Be careful where you put your cock. Put your cock somewhere safe.

[*He begins to sodomize her.*]

MAN. She looked like you, Sylvie. Like you. Sitting in the cafe with her French army man. Flirting with French army men. I'd never seen her before. If you had money, Sylvie, you would look like that. Dressed in black. High heels. Big hat. I brought her plate. Napkin on my arm. Stupid smile on my face. I've been trapped wanting you. You running to France.

SYLVIE. I'll stop wanting your song in my flesh. I'll stop knowing how to want.

MAN. Listen to what I'm telling you. The bomb blew her soldier to bits. Tore open her face. The bomb tore off her face. Blood everywhere. I lifted her up. Lifted her up while she died. I was as deep into her as I am into you. She died singing my song. Fancy French whore.

SYLVIE. My God. Oh, my God.

MAN. You'll never be free. You'll never be free of me. You've got my smell on your thighs. You've got my blood in your blood. You've got my sons.

SYLVIE. Shut up. You woke up Michel. With your dirty talk you woke up your son. Get back to bed, Michel. Get back to bed. Won't you ever leave me alone? If you tell Claude what you've seen, I'll wring your neck. You want your father? Here he is. Blood on his hands. Good for nothing but killing and having sex. You want to be like that? Is that what you want? He kills everything, Michel. Kills everything he's ever touched. You've got to forget how to want.

[*Michel's flashback ends. He is back in the present.*]

MICHEL. Hannah, can you come to me, now? Can you fly? Are you here with me, now? Are you here? Hannah, I need you in my life. You give me something I don't get. Don't leave me, Hannah. Hannah, don't leave me. I come back. I come back when I can. You know that. I come back. Hannah, I need you again.

[*Transition, now, to a scene imprinted in Hannah's unconscious.*]

CORA. I tried to do everything right. I didn't know what else to do. I didn't know how to cope. The child got sick. She got sick from it all. I went to my mother's house. Showed her my bruises, my cuts. I have a sick little girl. I have a sick child. And she turned her eyes. "This doesn't happen to our kind. This doesn't happen to women like us. Where would I put you and a child? I have my own life. Wear a high collar. Get him to buy you a fur. A fur with a cowl neck. Why did you marry an Italian man? Jews don't beat their wives. I love you and the child. I want you to do the right thing. It's a pity she's so dark. Looks just like him. Go home, Cora, go home. He makes good money. At least he does that. Be happy, Cora, with what you've got."

TONY. Baby, baby, your mother's gone. She's gone and left us alone. You're all I have, now. All I've got.

CORA. How you hold that child. So gentle. So close. How you rock her back and forth. Wipe her head with a cloth. She's the one, isn't she? She's the only one for you.

TONY. Cora, thank God. Thank God, you're back. I was frightened, Cora. I was scared. Cora, you look like an angel to me. The kid's asleep. Come on, Cora. I'll make you feel good.

CORA. No, Tony. Go on to bed. I want to stay here with the child.

TONY. I told you. She's asleep.

CORA. Go on, Tony. I'll sit awhile. I want to sit with the child. I want to sit with her, that's all. She's my child.

She's my little girl.

[*Cora sits. Hesitantly, she begins to sing a Yiddish lullaby to the sleeping child. Her quiet, cracked voice begins to be filled with the song. Tony watches for a while. Then he sits at her feet, his head in Cora's lap.*]

TONY. Baby, haven't I held you soft? Haven't I sung you to sleep?

[*Tony joins his voice to Cora's. They sing for a while. Then the memory vanishes. Hannah is back in the present.*]

HANNAH. Go on, now. Go. Go on, please. Either stay here forever with me or go back to your wife.

MICHEL. Because of you, Hannah, I go away full. I never want more. Then, in a few days or a week, I start longing again. Passion like ours Hannah, is worth the pain.

HANNAH. Michel, I don't want to see you again.

MICHEL. Hannah, why talk like this? We can still meet. I'll come to you when I can. You know that.

HANNAH. No, Michel. I need myself back.

MICHEL. Hannah, one day a week for an hour or two. What harm can come?

HANNAH. Michel, I can't tie myself up longing for you.

MICHEL. With passion like ours, Hannah, we have no choice.

HANNAH. No, Michel. I want to write it all down. While the smell still drips from my thighs and the ash coats my tongue, I want to give form. From perfect pain, perfect peace.

MICHEL. You're lying, Hannah. You're lying to me. You can't say "no." You don't know how. You'll be back. In a week or two or a month, you'll be calling me. Begging me to take you anyway I can.

HANNAH. No, Michel. Not this time. I've wanted you more than I have ever wanted anything. I wanted the past again. I wanted it all as it was. I wanted the start. To grow from the earth again. To be made new. Grown new on our love. I'm leaving you, Michel. I can't stay. I must go.

MICHEL. This is how you give, Hannah. This is how. You beg me to want you. You beg me. I do. I want you, Hannah. I want you. Now you step on me. Now you kill. I loved you, Hannah, I did. I loved you. But you had to hurt. You had to cut. You could never be happy with what you had. You never had enough. How does it feel, Hannah? Does it feel good? How does it feel to kill love?

[*Transition to Hannah's dream of her father. Michel fades from Hannah's life.*]

HANNAH. I dreamt of my father last night. He sat on a wooden bench spooning something into his mouth. What are you eating, Daddy, what?

TONY. Bone marrow from a can. I want to come back to you. I want it to be like it was.

HANNAH. I kissed him and he turned to ash. His flesh turned to ash on my tongue.

TONY. Baby, come closer to me. It's hard to hear. What are you saying to me?

HANNAH. What hurt you, Daddy, when you were young? I didn't know you then. What hurt you so bad?

TONY. Baby, baby, don't bother your head. Come on, let's go. You and me. Let's go for a ride.

HANNAH. You always looked so hurt to me. I wanted to help. I wanted to mend.

TONY. It's all right, babe. It's all right again. It will be like it was.

HANNAH. I kissed you and you turned to ash. Daddy, you're growing small. You're shrinking while we talk.

TONY. Baby, baby don't cry. Let's sneak outside. Let's go for a ride.

HANNAH. You're so small, I can swallow you whole. Swallow you up. I swallowed you whole. You churn in me, belly-full.

TONY. Baby, baby, don't go. Don't leave me alone.

THE END

Better People

A SURREAL COMEDY
ABOUT GENETIC ENGINEERING
AND REPRODUCTIVE TECHNOLOGY

CHARACTERS

The play alternates between the waking and dream lives of these four scientists:

DR. HAILA GUDENSCHMARTZER, very, very old, the senior woman geneticist in the nation; a refugee from Hitler

DR. EDWARD CHREODE, her son, also a geneticist

DR. PHILBERT WALLACE, Chair of the Molecular Biology Department at This Great University; president of Generecombo, Inc.; three-time winner of the Nobel Prize

DR. THEODORA FORENSIC, the first woman born of the genes of two male Nobel Prize–winning scientists; brilliant young post-doctorate assistant to Dr. Gudenschmartzer; later, head of her own laboratory

There then enters:

THE BEAST, a Yak with Kudoo horns; a rare, near-extinct species

And later:

THE BABY-BEAST, with the face of a human child, animal fur, and baby horns

SETTING

A single set represents the four laboratories of four geneticists in the Microbiology Department of This Great University, located somewhere on the East Coast. Stark and white, tall with sharp, surreal angles for walls. Four doors (two positioned against the back wall, one each on both side walls); the doors are also strangely shaped and are slightly small. Each small door is the doorway into the laboratory/office of a single scientist. The scientists' names are written backwards on their doors. One door has no name. After scene 5, it will become Theodora's. A set of oversized double doors is upstage right. The double doors exit into a large shared experimental laboratory, or operating room. In each scene, we enter the laboratory of the person whose door is used as an entrance. The hallway is behind the set. This set allows for seamless movement from scene to scene and its multiple doors enhance the comic and surreal aspects of the play. The set is rigged so that it can fall away, wall by wall, for the final transformation.

PROLOGUE

[The well-equipped, white laboratory is empty. An alarm goes off, as if there's been a leak of dangerous material in a lab. The siren sounds. Red lights blink off and on. The sound of scurrying feet. Of emergency showers. Inaudible, but alarmed voices. The first part of the prologue is played in slow motion. The mood is eerie, dreamlike. The scientists are dressed head-to-toe in white emergency suits. A door opens.]

SCIENTIST #1. Where? When?

[Exits. Another scientist enters from another door. Speaks:]

SCIENTIST #2. How? What do you mean?

[#2 exits. #3 enters one door, exits another.]

SCIENTIST #3. Impossible!

[#3 exits. #4 enters.]

SCIENTIST #4. Definite signs . . . warnings . . .

[#4 exits. The following dialogue takes place offstage.]

SCIENTIST #3. Impossible, I tell you.

SCIENTIST #1. Deadly . . .

SCIENTIST #3. Don't use that word . . .

SCIENTIST #4. [*Enters*] This is it, then . . .

SCIENTIST #2. [*Enters*] Call it back. Call it back now. Make it come home.

SCIENTIST #4. [*Enters*] New form of life. Can't call back.

SCIENTIST #3. [*Enters*] Statistically impossible!

SCIENTIST #1. Clean it up. Clean.

SCIENTIST #4. It's not toxic waste. It can't be cleaned up.

SCIENTIST #2. Grows on its own.

SCIENTIST #1. If the microecology of soil organisms is disrupted . . .

SCIENTIST #4. Catastrophic.

[*They freeze.*]

SCIENTIST #3. Won't anyone listen to me? Statistically impossible!

SCIENTIST #4. Nevertheless, some got out.

SCIENTIST #3. Statistics say, it didn't happen at all.

[*They freeze.*]

SCIENTIST #1. Plug the leak. Bring it back.

SCIENTIST #2. Shut the doors.

[*They break from slow-motion movement to frantically run around implementing the safety precaution devices in the lab.*]

SCIENTIST #3. Flush . . . put on the lid.

SCIENTIST #1. Turn up the heat.

SCIENTIST #3. Turn that heat down!

SCIENTIST #4. Rain. Rain will wash it away.

[*#4 breaks into "pagan" rain dance; #2 joins.*]

SCIENTIST #2. Sunlight. Sunlight will kill it.

SCIENTIST #4. Let's hope for a freeze.

[*They freeze.*]

SCIENTIST #1. Impossible to think . . . we, in this lab . . .

SCIENTIST #2. [*Sees something horrible*] Oh, my God. No. I don't believe this . . .

SCIENTIST #3. Listen to me, for God's sake. Couldn't have happened this way. It will die in the air. It won't multiply.

SCIENTIST #2. Multiply? Oh, shit.

SCIENTIST #3. Watch yourself. Don't leak a word of this leak.

SCIENTIST #4. We've done what we can.

SCIENTIST #3. Don't anyone talk.

[*They move together in a huddle.*]

SCIENTIST #2. We've taken every precaution.

SCIENTIST #4. Let's get back to work.

SCIENTIST #3. I'll handle the report.

SCIENTIST #2. Let's make up a bug that will eat it!

SCIENTIST #1,2,3,4. Yes, yes. There's work to be done. Deadlines to meet. Back to work. That's best. Eat it! Of course! Work, yes, work. Work, what a relief!

[*They shake hands. Hug. Return to their labs.*]

SCENE 1

[Edward Chreode enters his lab, proofing calculations on a long sheet of computer paper which trails behind him. Just as Chreode shuts the door with his foot, Philbert Wallace enters.]

PHILBERT. Edward, Edward, the results. Come on, man. You're the last to turn your work in.

[Edward gathers reams of computer printouts, hands them to Philbert.]

EDWARD. I can't say I'm sorry to see the end of this.

PHILBERT. The end of it! You haven't seen the beginning yet.

EDWARD. I suppose not.

PHILBERT. Aren't you proud? Aren't you thrilled? We've mapped the whole damn thing. It's our window into life. Everything we need to know . . . But I can't waste time now . . . so much hinges on my speech this afternoon.

EDWARD. We're all looking forward . . .

PHILBERT. You need inspiration, man, vision. A concrete sense of where we're going. You're not the only one. I just hope I've found the right words, the right tone. Edward, I hope I can pull this one off.

EDWARD. You'll be eloquent, I'm sure.

PHILBERT. Thanks, pal. It's so hard to know.

EDWARD. You'll be great.

[Philbert exits.]

EDWARD. Maybe I can find some time for my own work now that mess is out of here.

[Edward Chreode falls immediately to sleep at his lab bench.

He is dreaming. An old woman appears: his mother, Dr. Haila Gudenschmartzer, in a wheelchair. She points to a spot.]

DREAM

HAILA GUDENSCHMARTZER. Die for me. There. On the ground.

EDWARD CHREODE. Die? Mama, I don't know how to die.

HAILA. Yes, you do.

[*She hands him a glass laboratory jar she has held on her lap.*]

HAILA. Take your soul out of the jar.

[*He takes out red glop.*]

HAILA. Feed it to me.

[*He does. She eats.*]

EDWARD. Thank you, I feel much better, now.

HAILA. You feel relieved.

EDWARD. Yes. I feel light. Freed.

HAILA. Of course. You've given your soul to me.

EDWARD. You've stuffed yourself.

[*He wipes her mouth.*]

I used to love the chocolate traces hidden in the corners of your lips when you came home late from the lab. You looked so sweetly guilty then. Soul. It's an archaic concept, after all. A man doesn't actually have a soul. It's an idea. A thought. A chemical reaction in the brain. Odd how absolutely light I am. Untroubled now. Unburdened. Free, as I said. And you, Mama, how beautiful you look. Like a young girl. Let's dance.

HAILA. Yes, dance. Let's dance, Edward. Dance.

[*She rises delicately from the wheelchair, as if she were suddenly young again. Tango music. They tango passionately and talk.*]

HAILA. I wanted always to be young. I wished for a youth. That was all. Unfettered. Free. I wanted to be light of heart. I wanted beauty, adoration, love. Flowers delivered in white boxes. The moon shining on silk dresses. But I was pulled down. Destroyed. Made wise before I grew old.

EDWARD. That's over now. Over and done. All the betrayal. The loss. The wet cheek pressed against glass.

HAILA. I always only longed for gentleness. Gentleness and respect.

EDWARD. How I waited for you. How I waited to grow. Up. Large enough to hold you in my arms.

HAILA. There was always so much to do. So much needed to be done. To be thought. To be thought out. I sat alone at my bench. I knew how you cried. Do you think I didn't cry when life passed me by? I wanted peace, dignity, respect, lightness of heart, success. I wanted to be seen. Seen as I was. I wanted to win all the prizes. I wanted my theories accepted. I wanted the chair. The lab in my name. Dignity. Peace. Lightness of heart. I wanted love.

EDWARD. Here I am.

HAILA. All I ever wanted was gentleness.

EDWARD. Gentleness and respect.

HAILA. I won't let you go.

EDWARD. I know. You won't let me go.

[*He picks her up and carries her back to the wheelchair. Music stops. She is ancient again.*]

HAILA. Die for me. There on the ground.

EDWARD. Die? I don't know how to die.

HAILA. Yes, you do. There, on the ground. Where I can see.

EDWARD. I don't have to die. Not for you. I'm going out. I'm leaving the house.

HAILA. I have your soul. Your soul is mine.

EDWARD. Keep it. Who cares? I'm fine as I am. I'm light. I'm free. My soul would be upsetting to me.

HAILA. I have your soul in my mouth.

EDWARD. It's an archaic concept. "Soul." A man has no soul. He has his body, his mind. Information to process. Work to be done. He has what he controls. What he knows. He is what he is. What he can touch. What he can see. A man has no soul. Where would it be kept? It's insane. A meaningless concept. A useless word. "Soul." Absurd.

HAILA. I'm dying, my child.

EDWARD. No, Mama, don't. Don't do that.

HAILA. I'm dying. I am.

EDWARD. No. I won't let you go.

HAILA. I'm dying, now, with your soul in my mouth.

[*She slumps in her chair. He buries his head. Weeps.*]

EDWARD. Mama, Mama, come back.

HAILA. [*She pops up.*] Here I am. Back as you asked. Soul? It's gone. Swallowed whole. Down the hatch. No worry, now. Do what I ask. Be. Be for me.

[*She wheels her chair forward. In fact, Haila Gudenschmartzer has just come in the door. He wakes.*]

DREAM ENDS.

EDWARD. Mother! You're here.

HAILA. Let's go, Edward. We're late.

[*Edward Chreode wheels Haila Gudenschmartzer out the door.*]

SCENE 2

[The auditorium of This Great University, where the National Academy of Science is meeting. As a Distinguished Scientist takes his place behind the plexiglass podium and greets the assembled audience, Edward Chreode wheels his mother, Haila Gudenschmartzer, into a front row seat, among the audience.]

HAILA. Not here, Edward, not here. Over there.

EDWARD. Here?

HAILA. Three. We need three seats.

DISTINGUISHED SCIENTIST. May we have order, please, order. Ladies and gentlemen, Mr. President, distinguished members of the National Academy of Science, welcome to this auspicious gathering.

[*Applause.*]

This meeting marks a very special occasion. We gather together to celebrate the completion of the Human Genome Mapping Project. [*Applause.*] We now know the precise location and the complete DNA sequence of each of the 100,000 human genes. We can now write down in exact detail all the genetic instructions for making a complete human being. [*Applause, again. He holds up his hands for silence.*] Yes, ladies and gentlemen, I know, it's absolutely intoxicating.

[Throughout the scene, Haila makes her remarks and elicits responses as "under-talk" during the formal speeches of the scientists. The whispered dialogue is amplified and is delivered simultaneously with the speeches.]

HAILA. [*In a loud whisper*] Yes, drunk on power, they all are. [*Spotting a late arrival*] There she is! Stand up and wave to her, Edward! Theodora. Theodora Forensic, over here.

THEODORA FORENSIC. [*Stumbling across audience feet to them*] How terrible to be late. Forgive me, please. I was caught up in the lab.

HAILA. Theodora Forensic, my new postdoc, meet Edward Chreode, my son.

THEODORA. Dr. Chreode, I'm so very glad to meet you.

EDWARD. Dr. Forensic, my pleasure. Here, sit here. We've saved a seat on the other side of Mother.

THEODORA. Thank you. How kind of you, Dr. Gudenschmartzer. Have I missed much?

HAILA. The usual self-congratulatory clap-trap.

DISTINGUISHED SCIENTIST. Together scientific visionaries, venture capitalists, and the United States government joined forces to create what I think we must all agree is the most significant accomplishment of the twentieth century. The map of the human genome is the first step in affording us complete mastery over the human gene pool.

[*Applause.*]

HAILA. And what will they do now? Make better people.

THEODORA. Oh, yes. Don't you think so . . .

EDWARD. I think there's something essential we haven't even formulated yet.

HAILA. If that's what you really think, stop blathering about it, Edward, and get to work.

THEODORA. I'm afraid I don't follow what you're . . .

[*"Hush" sounds from the audience.*]

DISTINGUISHED SCIENTIST. Like the Manhattan Project of the 1940s, the Human Genome Project of the 1990s has put America first in the areas of visionary scientific breakthrough, major technological accomplishment, and renewed economic edge over the rest of the industrialized world.

HAILA. The Manhattan Project was the first scientific concentration camp in this country; this genome project has been the second.

EDWARD. Mother . . .

HAILA. Edward . . . you've done nothing for the past ten years but count proteins.

THEODORA. Dr. Chreode, how thrilling.

DISTINGUISHED SCIENTIST. Among the eminent research scientists who joined forces to complete this massive project in record time, no one man deserves our thanks more than Dr. Philbert Wallace.

[*Applause.*]

HAILA. Philbert Wallace is a self-serving fool.

EDWARD. Mother, please, you're not having breakfast with me — you're in a crowded room.

HAILA. Where I am does not alter the character of Philbert Wallace one slight bit.

EDWARD. Hush.

DISTINGUISHED SCIENTIST. Philbert Wallace, three-time Nobel Prize–winning scientist and Fortune 500 CEO who from his adjacent laboratories at This Great University and offices at Generecombo, Inc. directed the mapping of more of the human genome than any other senior researcher.

HAILA. I taught him everything he knows about science. I suppose his own mother is responsible for the corruption of his character.

THEODORA. Gene alteration is my special area of interest. Are you deeply involved, Dr. Chreode?

HAILA. He sequenced genes ad nauseum. It's miraculous his brain is still in working order.

EDWARD. Mother, for God's sake, you can't keep talking like this . . .

HAILA. Don't forget, I spoke up against Hitler in '34. I criticized his mad eugenics program then and I did my time in a camp because of it.

DISTINGUISHED SCIENTIST. Ladies and gentlemen, distinguished fellows of the National Academy of Science, may I present to you Dr. Philbert Wallace.

[*As the applause increases, and during the following dialogue, the actor who had played the Distinguished Scientist turns around and takes off mustache or beard, changes ties, etc., becoming Philbert Wallace. When the transformation is complete, he begins his speech.*]

HAILA. Our kind ought to be unworldly, monkish. Philbert's a master politician. It's dangerous.

EDWARD. Mother, please, this isn't Germany; it's not 1934.

HAILA. Philbert's had Congress eating out of his hands for the past 10 years, and they've eaten plenty of shit.

[*Enormous applause for Philbert Wallace. He holds up his hands for silence. Philbert Wallace speaks with studied confidence and a smooth, ingratiating manner. He has learned how to win an audience.*]

PHILBERT. My fellow colleagues in this great enterprise, thank you very much for your warm, enthusiastic welcome. You know, it's been said that a man has nothing until he has won the respect of his peers. If that's so, then I must be among the very richest men in the world.

HAILA. He's made a fucking fortune off of science.

EDWARD. Will you try to listen to Philbert's speech.

HAILA. The arrogance appalls me. The "human genome" as if there were some single one.

EDWARD. Yes, well did it ever occur to you that insults aren't terribly effective?

HAILA. Mark my words, Edward Chreode, mark my words. An entirely new theoretical formulation is what's needed.

EDWARD. That's exactly what I'm working toward. A new vision.

HAILA. Well, hurry up. And stop doing shit work for Philbert Wallace.

EDWARD. How else does one fund oneself?

PHILBERT. You know it wasn't always this way. I remember days and weeks and months of people telling me I was nuts, that the human genome couldn't be mapped, that we didn't have the technology necessary to master such a task. Then there were the arduous and depressing Congressional hearings spent answering our critics, the environmentalists, the feminists, the Catholic Church, even those few doubters within our ranks, people and organizations who for their own, I'm certain, honorable motives cling to the outmoded notion that human beings are not equipped to interfere with nature and that human knowledge itself ought to be limited.

Well, let me tell you something right here and now, human knowledge is not limitable. Human knowledge is a God given gift and we are here on this earth in order to carry out the greatest of all human projects, to join hands with nature, not against her, in the perfection of human life itself.

[*Applause.*]

THEODORA. Oh, I'm so excited to be sitting here, at this moment! Now that the genome has been mapped, human gene alteration is around the corner.

HAILA. Have you read any history along with all that science?

THEODORA. We're making history today.

HAILA. Regrettably.

EDWARD. Hush. He's about to acknowledge his colleagues.

HAILA. Memory. Memory! Where, in what gene, does the collective memory reside?

[*An amplified "shushhh," as if from all the people seated around Haila.*]

EDWARD. Mother, you've got to be quiet now.

PHILBERT. Now, let me tell you something you might not already know. I wasn't always a research scientist. No, once I was a humble resident on a hospital ward and I saw, day in and day out, the suffering of human beings. I saw cancer deaths, heart attack deaths, deaths by stroke, deaths from genetic diseases like Parkinson's, Huntington's, Cystic Fibrosis, Tae Sachs. One Christmas Eve, my esteemed friends and colleagues, I lost four beautiful children to the ravages of leukemia. The deaths of those four innocent children on Christmas Eve drove me into the lab, ladies and gentlemen, fellow scientists. The deaths of those four innocent babes led me to devote the rest of my life to the two-pronged task of curing and preventing genetic defects in our young. Yes, I promised myself I would not rest until the human genome had been mapped. And I have not rested and we have brought this project home a full five years ahead of schedule. [*Applause.*] And now that this enormous task has been accomplished, I want to renew my promise, in front of you and with you. I will not rest until the molecular biology community has learned how to prevent or to correct each and every terrible trick the human gene pool persists in playing on human beings.

Gene alteration is the ANSWER, ladies and gentlemen. Once we learn how to alter genes we will hold the future in our hands. Gene alteration will allow us to cure, in utero or in vitro, any of the over 10,000 genetic maladies that are currently detectable, and many other malfunctions we don't even label as diseases, yet. With gene alteration, every couple's natural longing to achieve the best possible genetic make-up for each of their offspring will become a glorious reality. Once parents, acting in concert with The Recombinant DNA Advisory Commission, are actually able to choose the physical and intellectual characteristics of their offspring, who can doubt that a world of gods and goddesses awaits us? With gene alteration techniques under our belts, we will have become impervious to illness, to defects, and, ultimately, even to death.

Our goal is nothing less than genetic perfection for every American. This and only this is the great work before us.

[*Deafening applause.*]

Thank you. Thank you. Thank you very much.

HAILA. Reach into my bag, Edward Chreode; I've brought some ripe tomatoes just for this very moment.

EDWARD. Mother, everyone we know is here. I won't let you humiliate yourself like this.

HAILA. Theodora, hand me my tomatoes.

[*The three of them begin to move out of the auditorium. Edward wheels his mother's chair across the floor in front of the stage, where the following dialogue is played.*]

THEODORA. It's so inspiring, isn't it, Dr. Chreode. Philbert Wallace is brilliant. Genetic Perfection. A disease-free world. Such a challenge is worth an entire lonely lifetime in a lab.

EDWARD. You've been bred to the task, haven't you?

THEODORA. You mean because I was born from two sperm inserted into an egg from which all the genetic material except the extra X had been previously removed. My fathers are feminist men. They made a bet with other less enlightened Nobel Prize winners that a woman might for once make a lasting mark on science.

HAILA. After all these years, my accomplishments aren't seen as major.

THEODORA. But, of course, I didn't mean to suggest . . . Your work on memory is supreme.

[*She bends enthusiastically over Haila's chair, paying homage.*]

You are the most highly esteemed woman scientist alive, Dr. Gudenschmartzer. That's why I'm here. I felt the need of a strong female influence since I never had a mother. I want to be a credit to my sex. I intend to perfect gene alteration techniques.

[*For a moment, Theodora, her hand on her breast, gazes out into her glorious future.*]

HAILA. Listen to her, Edward. You need guts like that.

THEODORA. But you were involved in the genome mapping project, weren't you, Dr. Chreode?

EDWARD. Call me Edward Chreode, please. My real work is something else. My wonderings are a bit diffuse right now. Difficult to pin down. But the speculations are endlessly fascinating. I do believe I'm on to something.

THEODORA. Could you introduce me to Dr. Wallace, Dr. Chreode? Gene alteration is the way to go. I have some rather concrete ideas for experiments.

HAILA. She'll marry the first Nobel Prize winner who asks her. She'll get money, patronage, a lab of her own; it all comes attached to his penis. And you, Edward, will never find a brilliant wife until you win the Prize.

EDWARD. Mother, I'm certain Dr. Forensic and I . . .

HAILA. [*Ignoring Edward, to Theodora*] I created Edward Chreode by myself. He's fatherless. So that I might present a masculine antidote to their pseudo-scientific twaddle and gibberish. A compassionate man with a brain. That's what I meant him to be.

[*Edward wheels his mother offstage; Theodora follows. The rest of the speech is heard as if it took place in the hall leading to the laboratory doors.*]

A feelingful soul with a speculative flare. Edward, my dear, self-assertion comes so very hard to you. But now the time has come for you to take a bold stab at a theory, publish, make yourself known. Wheel me back to the lab. Edward, Theodora, I feel the blood begin to thunder in my veins. We have important work ahead.

[*Theodora opens the door to Haila's lab.*]

SCENE 3

[Haila Gudenschmartzer is wheeled in the door of her lab by Theodora Forensic. Haila is still talking.]

HAILA. I am locating the exact spot where memory is stored within the brain. I am very, very close to the solution, now.

[Haila holds up some papers containing research results. Theodora eyes them eagerly as she shuts the door with one hand. Philbert opens the door just as she shuts it.]

PHILBERT. Haila, I need your ear.

[Haila quickly hides her research. Theodora gapes at Philbert, her "hero," but sees she is not expected to stay as Haila waves her away and she exits awkwardly.]

HAILA. Pah. Philbert Wallace. When did you ever need anything from me? Except my knowledge and that you have pilfered, Philbert, to use for your own greed.

PHILBERT. You're the best teacher I ever had. I'm your protégé.

HAILA. The best teacher of the biggest genetic mogul in the nation is struggling away, as always, in an under-equipped laboratory, underfunded, understaffed, under-respected.

PHILBERT. Haila, gene alteration is around the corner. I need your enthusiastic endorsement of my research program.

[Philbert takes the endorsement paper from his right lab coat pocket, flourishes it at her. She waves it away; she isn't going to sign.]

HAILA. I thought your speech was a piece of shit, by the way.

PHILBERT. Always the kind word from you, Haila, always the kind word. You'll never understand how much your disapproval hurts me.

HAILA. I've offended you, Philbert, that's why my grants don't come through?

PHILBERT. I always vote in your favor. I'm a loyal man, Haila. Let's face it, you haven't been hot for awhile.

HAILA. I've always been hot, Philbert. And you've always known how hot I've always been.

PHILBERT. Your lab is almost out of money. It's been a long time since you published anything. Now, if you don't want to turn your attention to gene alteration, it might finally be just the right moment for you to retire. I'll plan the festivities myself. Retire in style, o.k.?

[*Philbert puts the endorsement paper back into his pocket.*]

HAILA. Bullshit, Philbert. You ask that young genius who has just apprenticed herself to me. She understands better than any of you how close I am to solving the secret of memory BY MYSELF. When I publish my results in a few months you won't even bother to read what I've found. I'm a woman. What could I know? I might even have been menstruating, polluting my results with unclean blood. That's how scientific you and your woman-hating tribe are. I still do menstruate, by the way, Philbert. I like the smell of menstrual blood. I still menstruate because I'm still fertile. Not a one of you read the paper explaining how I accomplished that. You're too busy making babies in Petrie dishes.

PHILBERT. What did you say, Haila?

HAILA. I still menstruate. I still bleed.

PHILBERT. I'll take you out for dinner. You can tell me about your private life. Right now, let's talk science. Let's talk brain, mind, memory. At the Top of the Sixes, I'll get us a nice table. You can continue your feminist diatribe over the beef. Maybe my speech was a little general, after all. I wasn't altogether pleased. Maybe I should have come right out and said all we need from the whole messy process are the eggs. Now what did you say about memory?

HAILA. You keep your hands off of my eggs, Philbert Wallace. I can still conceive quite nicely on my own. Give birth naturally and be back in the lab, the kid strapped to my belly, within a week. I would prove it to you, if I was able to find a man with genetic and moral fiber equal to my own. But you all have always been swine. In a month, I'll understand human memory.

PHILBERT. Haila, if you weren't such a damn fine scientist I'd never be able to put up with you.

HAILA. In a month, I'll know exactly *where and how* memory is stored within the brain. I'm on the verge of understanding everything.

PHILBERT. That's the stuff, Haila. Get me a full report today. I'll put you on full retainer at Generecombo, Inc.

HAILA. Don't patronize me, young man. Give me the money I need because of my brilliant mind.

[*Triumphantly, Haila hands him the proof, her research results. He takes the papers, reads; becomes convinced and excited. Immediately he's off into his own world of products and profits.*]

PHILBERT. The control of human memory. That's marketable. We win the public's sympathy by offering it up as a cure for Alzheimer's disease (which I forgot, by the way, to mention in my speech). An ethics committee will be convened by the boys in Congress. Who is worthy of having a memory, that sort of thing. Meanwhile, who can resist? It's science. It's progress. It's truth. Haila, I knew you'd come through for me in the end.

[Philbert offers his hand for her to shake. She refuses, swings her chair away.]

HAILA. Not so fast, Philbert Wallace, I want the Nobel Prize for this. My life's work. I want to die with the Prize in my hand. I want my eggs frozen alongside all that sperm in the Nobel sperm bank. I want equality at last.

PHILBERT. Haila, I'm offering you millions.

HAILA. I want the Prize, Philbert.

[Pause. He looks at the results again. Decides.]

PHILBERT. O.k., o.k. I'll see what I can do.

HAILA. So you think I'm hot, at last, Philbert.

PHILBERT. Haila, there's no one in science whose integrity and accomplishments I admire more. You've stuck to the good, hard, theoretical work; you've never profiteered off of science. You're a well-known supporter of liberal causes; you're an old line feminist, a refugee from Hitler, and a single mother to boot. You've got principles, Haila. You deserve the Nobel Prize. I'm glad to have you on our team.

[He offers his hand, again. This time she takes it. They shake.]

HAILA. And you, Philbert, are a slippery, self-important penis who was badly toilet trained. But, I'm glad to be included on your team.

PHILBERT. With the Prize under your belt, you will finally be taken seriously.

[He puts her research paper into his left lab coat pocket then takes a contract from his inside jacket pocket, flourishes it in front of her.]

PHILBERT. This is Generecombo's standard option agreement. It gives the company complete rights to market any and all memory control products we invent based upon your pure research. It also gives you quite a handsome advance.

[*Philbert pencils a large $ figure into the contract. Hands it to her.*]

PHILBERT. Sign it.

[*Haila reads quickly, signs. He takes it back.*]

PHILBERT. And, Haila, no more displays like the one I witnessed at my speech.

[*He comes quite close to her.*]

You may humiliate me in private only.

[*He pulls back and begins to pace.*]

You know, Haila, I was disappointed in my speech, myself. It lacked nerve. The truth is I got scared. I cut out the most radical part. I had intended to offer a concrete gene maximization plan. I was going to suggest that we simply remove the genetic material from each individual immediately after birth and then promptly sterilize that individual. The idea's been around for a long time, of course. During each individual's lifetime, record would be kept of accomplishments and characteristics. After the individual's death, a committee decides if those genes are worthy of procreation into other individuals. If so, genetic material would be removed from the depository, mated suitably, and implanted into a surrogate. If not, the genetic material is destroyed. How simple, elegant, direct. But at 3 a.m., I cut the paragraph out. I shouldn't have done that, should I?

[*But Haila has fallen asleep in her chair.*]

PHILBERT. Haila, are you listening? That old trick again. What a pig-headed, impossible woman.

[*He whispers to her sleeping face.*]

You had better not make a fool out of me, Haila. You had better come through; I've invested in you.

[Philbert exits in a huff; DREAM music and lights. Haila rises out of her wheelchair and exits through the large double doors.]

DREAM

[Eduard Schneider, played by the actor who plays Edward Chreode, sits weeping in the middle of Haila's dream. He is talking, as if he is a split personality, to himself.]

EDUARD SCHNEIDER. Don't cry, Edward.

EDWARD CHREODE. Why shouldn't I cry? I wanted to be like other people. I'm not like them at all.

EDUARD SCHNEIDER. It's wrong to cry about that. You can't help the way you are.

EDWARD CHREODE. Other people have inner lives. They have places they can get to. Places they can hide. Other people have private thoughts.

EDWARD SCHNEIDER. Yes, Edward. Be proud. You've been asked to give up so much. You can live without an inner life.

EDWARD CHREODE. But I must cry. I must grieve. I must mourn.

EDUARD SCHNEIDER. Buck up, Edward. You still look fine. It's important to pretend. Think of your grandmother. No one ever knew she was a Jew.

EDWARD CHREODE. All my life, I've pretended to do the right thing. But I'm not what they say. I remember when I could see the whole distance round the world. I had the whole vision, then. I saw everything.

EDUARD SCHNEIDER. So what. Do you think anyone cares about you?

EDWARD CHREODE. Why do you make me cry? What's the

purpose in that. If I cry, I can't feel anything. And I used to have feelings of my own.

EDUARD SCHNEIDER. Shut up, Edward. Don't go soft on me. That sort of talk is better unheard. You're not like other people, Edward. You do what you're told. You give what you're asked. You sacrifice.

EDWARD CHREODE. No. Stop. I had an idea. I had a thought. A thought came into my head. This time, this time, I am going to try. I am going to try to show who I am.

[Eduard Schneider writes his letter.]

Dear Herr Doktor Wirths:

"I must refute this charge of imbecility with schizophrenic tendencies, since I am capable of writing and of doing arithmetic without error and without outside help. For this reason, I would like to request another physical examination."

[*Dr. Wirths (played by the actor who plays Philbert Wallace) enters with Haila, playing herself as a young woman. Dr. Eduard Wirths was soon to become one of the chief doctors, i.e., killers at Auschwitz. Tall, handsome Aryan looks, he is also bizarrely gentle and kindly (as indeed the real Wirths was known for his compassionate care of patients, even as he oversaw the killing of millions.) A committed Nazi, devoted husband and father, Wirths believes he is doing his duty purifying the German race. In other words, Wirths is the true split personality, the killer/doctor in one body. Haila's dream memory intensifies these characteristics; Wirth's split is boldly portrayed.*]

WIRTHS. Good morning, Herr Schneider.

[*He takes the letter, pockets it.*]

WIRTHS. I have received your most impressive letter. Fraulein Doktor will perform another examination on you. Sterilize him, Fraulein. Inject this caustic substance through the urethra. It will block the testes. Check him in a week. If gangrene has set in, amputate. Don't be afraid, Herr Schneider. You see, I've brought you a beautiful young woman doctor. What could possibly go wrong? She'll be won completely over by your charm. Sterilize him, now, Fraulein.

[Wirths exits.]

EDUARD SCHNEIDER. You are a nice lady. I can see that.

HAILA. Don't count your chickens before they hatch.

EDUARD SCHNEIDER. That's just it. I can't help doing that. Everyone must. It's human. I feel that it is. I don't want to be sterilized.

HAILA. Whoever put that idea into your head? I've come to speak with you a bit, take your blood, and do a sperm count. Here, masturbate into this jar.

EDUARD SCHNEIDER. I'm not as young as I was. Well, maybe I will never marry. I wanted to marry this year. Maybe the woman I love will not want to marry me. I wouldn't marry except for love. I know how to love, I do.

HAILA. I've had 39 lovers. I've given myself five abortions. I've cured myself three times of pelvic inflammatory disease and of countless yeast infections. I'm the last woman in Berlin who remembers the erotic life.

EDUARD SCHNEIDER. It's because they found out I have a Jewish grandmother. That's why they are doing this. I'm not stupid, you know. I'm no dumber than lots of them in uniform.

HAILA. I had a Jewish lover, once. But he asked for too much.

EDUARD SCHNEIDER. Maybe you have been hurt in love. Too many times. I'm a dairy herdsman. I work with cows. But I've got my dreams.

HAILA. Yes, yes, you can dream.

EDUARD SCHNEIDER. You know, I thought, if we two could talk. If we could share, well, you won't be able to do what they want done.

HAILA. I'm here on orders. Routine examination only.

EDUARD SCHNEIDER. I could love a woman. I know I could.

HAILA. You're not done. Quickly, finish up before he comes back. It's a simple mechanical thing. I just need a sperm count. We are doing a comparison rating. Do Jewish men produce more sperm? It's pure science. Pure research.

EDUARD SCHNEIDER. I believe the amount of sperm produced must have to do with the amount of love felt. I believe it's the passion at the moment of conception which determines the joy in the soul of the unborn.

HAILA. Now then, I just must give you this injection.

[*She injects his penis with the caustic substance. Sound of machine gun fire. His body reacts in a spasm to the pain.*]

EDUARD SCHNEIDER. No, no, why did you have to do that? I begged you. I pleaded with you. I looked into your eyes. I shared my dreams. I believed in tenderness. I believed in love.

HAILA. Buck up, Eduard Schneider. Buck up. These are hard times. None of us does what we want. We are struggling to stay alive. Go home. Forget about this.

EDUARD SCHNEIDER. You expect me to forget?

HAILA. Look, I've saved your sperm. They wanted to destroy it.

[*Haila looks at the (imaginary) sperm jar. "Why did I save this?" she silently asks herself. Then she* **knows.**]

HAILA. I'm going to have a child with this. I'm going to inject myself. I will sex select. I will make a son. A noble, gentle, brilliant man. A boy-child with your soul, my brains. I've had counts, classicists, artists, actors, professors of chemistry, biology, physics, poetry, history, politicians and judges, psychiatrists. You are the only man I've desired a child with.

EDUARD SCHNEIDER. What will become of him? What will become of my son? He missed out from the start. Never to feel the shock of collision between egg and sperm. Never to feel the light of my love? How I sought him everywhere with every thrust, never to hear my shout, my shout of triumph when he was formed?

[*Wirths returns.*]

WIRTHS. Finished, Fraulein, I hope.

HAILA. Yes. Everything is as you wished.

WIRTHS. We killed two birds with one stone.

[*Wirths sends Eduard Schneider's wheelchair rolling towards the double doors, Schneider disappears.*]

WIRTHS. An idiot and a Jew. It must make you feel proud, Fraulein, to be a woman in 1934, at the forefront of eugenic science. I'm going to recommend you for promotion. There are some very interesting experiments soon to begin at several major hospitals here in Berlin. We will soon have access to unlimited experimental material. We are entering a golden age of science. Of racial purification and advanced reproductive techniques. I'm going to recommend a transfer and a promotion for you.

[*Haila falls back into her chair, jerks awake, screams.*]

[DREAM ENDS]

HAILA. Edward! Edward, my son!

[*Edward rushes in. Like many children of concentration camp survivors, he's been through camp nightmares many times before.*]

EDWARD. You're not in the camps, Mother, you're here, in the lab, with me.

HAILA. The beatings. My back. My back. The horrible pressure on my spine.

EDWARD. It's all over now.

HAILA. I ran, I ran. For the last time, I walked by myself.

EDWARD. You're safe in the lab with me.

HAILA. Why, Edward, is it always pain? Pain so vivid, biting at us?

EDWARD. Calm, Mother, calm.

[*Suddenly, she wakes fully out of her dream. Haila is fully present. An important new thought has come into her head because of the dream and waking moment she just had.*]

HAILA. Edward, I've been wrong. Memory cannot be stored solely in the brain. Memory is lodged in the flesh. The body, the organs, the cells, the hormones, the glands feel the memory first, before we are conscious of it.

[*She pauses for a moment, following this thought through to its next question.*]

HAILA. But where has the memory been, Edward? Tell me that. Where is memory kept? In the body, itself, or somewhere else? Leave me, now, go. I must think it through.

SCENE 4

[*Edward Chreode enters his lab and begins to work. Philbert Wallace enters just behind.*]

PHILBERT. Hallo, Edward.

EDWARD. Philbert, come in. A most impressive speech.

PHILBERT. That's not what your mother said.

EDWARD. You know Mother, a most difficult one.

PHILBERT. Listen, pal, I've got a plum for you. Huge contract. Major grant.

EDWARD. Philbert, that's very kind.

PHILBERT. Fortunately, I'm in a position to take care of my own.

EDWARD. I'm honored, touched.

PHILBERT. Edward, you're in line for promotion, at last. Only . . . you've hardly published a thing. You're not very good at getting grants.

EDWARD. Well, perhaps. Philbert, I'm thinking out a major theory. It's slow work, not easy.

PHILBERT. Edward, I, for one, have faith in you.

EDWARD. Philbert, I'm onto something BIG.

PHILBERT. How would you like a small fortune for research? Prestige? An inside track on what's happening, what's hot?

EDWARD. Well, of course . . .

PHILBERT. Fascinating research. Necessary to the U.S. You can do your own thing on the side. Which, by the way, is what?

EDWARD. Thoughts far-ranging. Problems of creation and form, mysteries of epigenesis, of regeneration, embryological speculations. How does form come into being for the first time? Why can certain damaged organs grow again? Biology's unsolved problems. Recently, I can't quite tell you why, I've become rather obsessed with the problem of extinction. What happens to the life force of the extinct, or soon to be so?

PHILBERT. What sort of question is that? Life force, it's an archaic concept.

EDWARD. Your speech led me to thinking that we ought to prepare for future extinctions by freezing the genetic material of endangered species so that we might regenerate them in future times, under more auspicious environmental conditions.

PHILBERT. Perfect, Edward. How soon can you get some general papers out? I'll see they're placed in the environmental magazines. We need precisely this sort of visibility at This Great University. It provides you with a perfect cover.

[*Edward is thrilled. Philbert moves in very close.*]

PHILBERT. Edward, we need your help manufacturing a new, lethal virus (as a vaccine, of course, as an antidote, not, according to Geneva, to be used as a first strike) for the Department of Defense. Will you say "yes?"

EDWARD. I don't think I really could consider that.

PHILBERT. A great deal is at stake. Personally, professionally, and for our country.

EDWARD. This stuff is dangerous. It's cultured in the *E. coli* bacterium which lives quite naturally in the human intestine. What if it got out?

PHILBERT. We build safety doors. Better you be the one than someone less environmentally inclined.

EDWARD. Oh, I don't know about that. My mind, at present, is quite occupied.

PHILBERT. This DOD contract will fund your passion, man. If I might be frank, there's no way the problems you just outlined will bring in the grants, not with the current administration. No way the current faculty can grant you the promotion. In contrast, slipping a little lethal virus into the *E. coli* bacterium might help us understand gene alteration! Be altruistic, if you wish. Your country needs you. Stop thinking always of yourself. For us, here at This Great University, a contract from the DOD is not to be sneezed away. Take an hour to think it over. I'll pop in again.

[*Philbert exits. Edward, disappointed and confused, sits down at his desk where he falls immediately asleep.*]

DREAM MUSIC & LIGHTS

[*Haila comes racing in madly in her wheelchair, beginning the* **DREAM IMAGE.**]

HAILA. Edward, I need, I need, I need. I have needs, Edward Chreode, needs. I have needs which must be met.

EDWARD. Yes, yes, of course.

HAILA. Give me your legs, Edward Chreode. I need them for mine.

[*He sits heavily on useless legs. She rises and walks.*]

HAILA. You must grab opportunity when it knocks. I rose to the top. By hard work, sacrifice, good common sense. Love, there was no room for love. I had lovers, I had plenty of those. But they couldn't stand on their own.

EDWARD. I can, Mama, I can stand up.

[*He tries to pull himself up by holding onto her. She brushes him off. He falls.*]

HAILA. They used me, each one. Weaklings. Sapped my strength.

EDWARD. Don't give your legs away, Edward Chreode. No, next time, I won't. I didn't really give them up. Not my own two feet. I kept my feet for myself. Legs can regenerate. It's a marvelous fact. The damaged organ regrows itself. Cut it off. It comes back. Grows again. Cut it off. It returns. What a marvelous fact.

HAILA. Edward, give me your head. I want to think a thought worthy of me through to the end.

[*Edward Chreode's head goes limp on his neck.*]

HAILA. It was always so difficult simply to be. To be strong. To be self-willed, purposeful. Not to succumb.

PHILBERT. Will you shut up, Haila. Your son let lethal bacteria leak from his lab. Three hundred thousand innocent civilians are expected to die.

HAILA. Is Edward all right? Did Edward survive?

EDWARD. [*Crawls to her*] Mama, I have collected their genes. The genes of all the condemned are in glass jars underground.

PHILBERT. Luckily, the undernourished, over-medicated, drugged, and despised will be first to succumb. Assure the population at large that everything's fine.

EDWARD. Out back, beneath the cement, I've stored all their traits. We will recreate each last one. Babies in their cribs. Octogenarians. Lovers entwined in their beds. I've stolen their genes to make them again.

THEODORA. [*Carrying a baby doll*] Look at my child. She's dead. She died.

EDWARD. Oh, my God, did you take out her genes? Did you save one of her eggs?

THEODORA. She was a test tube baby. Do you know how long I worked to make her? Do you have any idea of what I went through?

PHILBERT. Call in the press. This is a perfectly acceptable level of environmental distress.

THEODORA. I'm going to sue. She was a perfect child. Blond, blue-eyed. High I.Q.

HAILA. We need protest marches, boycotts, riots. A good disaster rouses the blood.

PHILBERT. Half a million have died. The plague is spreading. The DOD wants no part of this. We need a high-toned memorial meeting. We need some good public grieving.

EDWARD. I will make her, again. I swear. Perfect as she was before.

THEODORA. Five procedures to flush the eggs out. Five punctures of the vaginal wall. Hundreds of diagnostic tests. Hormones, minerals, vitamins, sonograms, scans, bed rest.

EDWARD. On my honor, as a man of my word, I will recreate each lost life, from their own genetic material which I have carefully stored in the backyard. I just have to crawl out there. I just have to dodge the lethal bacteria. I knew something would happen someday. We all knew it, didn't we? That's why I collected their genes. The genes of the innocent ones. I stored them in a deep freeze. Next to the orange popsicles.

HAILA. Nothing like a disaster to bring people together. Now they'll understand how stupid, lethargic, weak-minded, deluded they have been all along. Trusting science to set it right! Take it from someone who knows the field. It's idiotic. Absurd.

PHILBERT. The DOD can't be bothered with this.

EDWARD. If only I had my legs back. If only I had the use of my head.

HAILA. Yes, we organized. We resisted. In the camps, underground. We refused. We suffered for our ideals.

PHILBERT. The DOD wants a whitewash. A sex scandal in the White House.

THEODORA. Fetal heart monitors. Cesarean. Neo-natal intensive care. Hundreds of thousands of team hours, dollars. What a blessing she was. What a right.

EDWARD. If I could only think straight. Maybe I could remember how they all were, rushing around. I can put them back just like that. They will regenerate.

HAILA. Come, come, Edward, screw your head on straight. Get off your behind. There's work to be done. Disaster is challenge for those who move fast. Seize opportunity when it knocks. You won't be their dupe. You'll know what to do. You'll use them. They won't use you.

[*Haila falls back into her chair and wheels herself out. Edward wakes abruptly.*]

DREAM ENDS.

[*Philbert Wallace enters.*]

PHILBERT. So, Edward, what do you say? It's a tasty offer, isn't it?

EDWARD. Philbert, don't be upset. I really think not.

PHILBERT. Don't be a fool, Edward, don't destroy your career.

EDWARD. It's really not in my line.

PHILBERT. Your country needs you, Edward.

EDWARD. *E. coli* can live in the human intestine. If it were to escape . . .

PHILBERT. You alter the strain, make it weak.

EDWARD. What about the probability of adaptive mutation?

PHILBERT. Edward, for God's sake, lighten up. What's life without risk? If I thought the way you do, I'd never get out of bed.

EDWARD. Plague is possible.

PHILBERT. Possible. Possible. Are you seriously suggesting we halt the progress of the scientific effort because something awful might result?

[*Pause. They look at one another. Edward doesn't know how to answer this line of thought.*]

PHILBERT. This research is necessary . . . not only to the DOD but to us, here, in this laboratory. Gene alteration techniques might hinge on what you learn. Do you understand? Edward, I'm making you my right hand man.

EDWARD. But reasonable caution.

PHILBERT. Reasonable caution, fine, fine. I like your approach, Edward. You're careful, you're steady, you're sure. Don't louse yourself up, Edward. How explicit do you expect me to be?

EDWARD. I'd want to take every precaution. No one would know what we're doing.

PHILBERT. My secret and yours. We're going to find out some crucial information. Let the DOD pay for it. *Our real work is to end human suffering.*

EDWARD. Well, Philbert, put like that . . . How could I . . . I owe you so much.

PHILBERT. I'll go ahead and notify the DOD. You can start culturing the new virus immediately. And, Edward, exercise caution. This stuff is dangerous.

SCENE 5

[*The double-doors swing open; Haila and Theodora Forensic are in the midst of a serious conversation. Haila is filled with excitement; Theodora is worried, depressed.*]

HAILA. So, memory *is not* stored within the brain.

THEODORA. But you've invalidated years of your own research.

HAILA. Now we go out again, into the unknown.

THEODORA. But an entirely new set of experiments needs to be thought through.

HAILA. Naturally. How thrilling.

THEODORA. But I don't have the slightest idea where to start.

HAILA. Ask yourself. Where can memory hide do you suppose?

THEODORA. But . . .

HAILA. This is science, my dear. Constant ignorance. Constant bliss . . . because what we will discover now will be far more beautiful than what we have disowned.

[*Haila wheels herself back out the double doors.*]

THEODORA. Bosh. Just when I thought I'd have more time for my own research.

[*The phone rings. Theodora is clearly exhausted; she's been trying to keep up with Haila's changing demands plus pursue her own research at night. Throughout the following phone call, she chews ravenously on a squished candy bar she finds in her lab coat pocket.*]

THEODORA. Yes. Yes. This is she. I know. I know. I'm sorry. I know. Still, it does not seem to me that three, even four or five first trimester abortions are too great a price a pay to achieve a perfect baby, if you still want a genetically connected child. [*Silence.*] But you are carrying defective genes. Abort, wait two months. Try again. [*Silence.*] Yes, I know the *Times* did report my astonishing success, but that was with mice.

[*Philbert Wallace opens the door a crack, stops to listen to the phone call.*]

THEODORA. The press exaggerates. [*Silence.*] No, it has nothing to do with cost. Look, I don't have my own lab. It's even difficult for me to talk. The technology has not been perfected yet. I have no time. [*Silence.*] I'll phone you in for the abortion. Try again. [*Silence.*] You can always go the surrogacy route. Implant a healthy egg and sperm. There is no longer any worry about custody suits; you can use a brain-dead fetal nurturer. They're reporting great success utilizing these neomorts. [*Silence.*] I'll get you a list of available wombs on life support systems. Think over your options. [*Silence.*] Crying won't help.

[*Philbert Wallace enters.*]

THEODORA. Someone's just come in, I must get off the line. Make yourself some tea. Read a book. Go shopping.

[*She hangs up the phone, throws her clipboard down on the floor.*]

THEODORA. Women! She's set herself up as a broodmare.

PHILBERT. You know how it is, Theodora, for a woman the need to procreate is all.

THEODORA. No, Philbert. I don't know how it is. The need to procreate doesn't show itself in me. The need to master gene therapy — that I feel. If I could get inside this weeping woman, now, with a needle, and stick a good gene on so she could have her perfect child in peace! That, Philbert, would be my destiny fulfilled.

PHILBERT. And you will, Theodora. Patience. Perseverance.

THEODORA. It's so damn frustrating, Philbert, to know so much . . .

[*Her glasses off, she stares, nearsightedly, into Philbert's face. They gaze at one another.*]

PHILBERT. Odds are one among us will figure it out, this year or next.

[*Philbert begins to move towards her; Theodora backs away from him, as he moves her around the table.*]

PHILBERT. Too many of us are right on the verge. Our business is simply to make certain the final breakthrough happens here. In these laboratories.

[*They end standing close together in the middle of the room. Philbert whispers seductively.*]

PHILBERT. Theodora, you need money, technicians, peace of mind.

[*Theodora is thrilled.*]

THEODORA. Oh, yes, Philbert, I do. I do. That's exactly what I need!

[*He continues coming towards her, and she backs across the room to the wall.*]

PHILBERT. I can give you that.

[*She is ecstatic. He keeps coming at her, backing her up against the wall.*]

PHILBERT. Then once we get gene therapy under our belts, we'll be set. For those who can pay the price, there will be no limits to perfectibility of the race. The human gene pool will be ours to endlessly manipulate. Of course, selective abortion will always be cheaper, easier.

[He falls on his knees in front of her, his arms pinned to the wall on either side of her.]

PHILBERT. Theodora, You possess the perfect genes and so do I. Together we can make a dynasty. Will you marry me?

[She leaps in fright.]

THEODORA. Philbert, please get up. I can't marry yet. I haven't proven myself.

[She gets away from him. He follows her, until during this speech he has backed her into the table. She leans back on the table and he comes down on top of her, as if to kiss her.]

PHILBERT. I'll set you up in your own laboratory. You'll be in complete control of your life.

Face it, Theodora, human gene alteration therapy is for those with flaws. But among the intellectual elite, genetic perfection already exists. We can become the models for everyone else.

[Just before his lips reach hers, Philbert pulls away. He goes upstage to the blackboard to illustrate his plan. Theodora sits, stunned, listening to him.]

PHILBERT. Here's my plan. We scrape a mere ten eggs per month off of your uterus, after multiple ovulation has been induced with injected drugs. We can fertilize those ten eggs in vitro with my sperm, collected fresh, or if I am feeling overworked, from the frozen stock already deposited in the Nobel sperm bank. Each zygote would be cultured to the blastocyst stage in vitro and screened for any unforeseen mutation before being implanted into a surrogate class of women, created from our immigrant or homeless populations, or, as you just said, from our newly dead. Unburdened, Theodora, by childbearing, you would keep on making your genetic contributions to succeeding generations. Practiced monthly for 25 years, the strategy I've just outlined would produce 2,910 offspring. I know that isn't much. But coupled with the efforts of an internationally select group of gene donors equal in stature to ourselves, a small, but powerful genetically elite intelligentsia could be created in our lifetime. Think of how humanity would benefit.

[*Philbert comes back to her, kneeling again in front of her.*]

PHILBERT. Theodora, be my wife. I adore you. I want to enter the gene pool with you.

[*Haila wheels herself in, recklessly.*]

HAILA. Philbert, get up from that ridiculous position. I need to speak with my assistant.

PHILBERT. I want you for eternity. I'll set you up in your own laboratory.

HAILA. Cut the crap, Philbert. You want to use her brains to speed your own research. But she's my post doc.

PHILBERT. She's perfect. Look at her. I feel the way Dante felt for Beatrice. It's not her brains I want. She can keep them for herself. I promise her intellectual freedom and respect. By the way, Haila, I need your memory work. The market research boys are getting antsy.

THEODORA. [*Looking at the paper Haila has handed her*] But, Haila, these experiments will keep us busy for years!

HAILA. Then we'd better get started, hadn't we?

PHILBERT. Theodora, a lab of your own.

[*He exits.*]

HAILA. Philbert, you're a thief.

THEODORA. He's asked me to marry him and give him all my eggs.

HAILA. And set you up in your own lab.

THEODORA. Yes.

HAILA. Are you ready for your own lab? That's the real question. Not whether you love him, which you don't.

THEODORA. Of course, I don't love him.

HAILA. But he'd make you a powerful, well-funded woman.

THEODORA. Yes.

HAILA. You can always take a lover in your spare time.

THEODORA. I don't have spare time. I need three years of funding and peace of mind.

HAILA. And, so, you would abandon me at this crucial moment?

THEODORA. But, Haila, I have to solve gene alteration techniques . . . Your memory work is . . .

HAILA. Can't those famous fathers of yours set you up in a funded lab?

THEODORA. Their bet was I could make it on my own.

HAILA. Marry Philbert, then. He'll support your work, and he won't distract you with his emotional needs. Philbert's completely blocked.

THEODORA. At least he doesn't want sex.

HAILA. When I was your age, I used to have my lovers in the lab. Make love, take a bath, do an experiment, make love. I'm the last woman alive who remembers the erotic life.

THEODORA. The erotic life doesn't interest me. I must get back to work. Can Edward drive you home? It's late.

HAILA. Don't stay all night.

[*Theodora falls immediately to sleep at her lab bench.*]

DREAM IMAGE

[Voices of Scientists on tape. Their large, grotesque shapes are seen through the plexiglass windows of the large double door. As Theodora lies sleeping on the table, her belly grows large. She wakes, very pregnant, stands drowsily, rubbing her big belly.]

VOICE. Alright, that's it. Here's to a job well done. The Caucasian gene pool is officially declared free of defect.

VOICE. Wait, what's that bleep on the screen?

VOICE. That's Theodora Forensic.

VOICE. She got herself pregnant by natural means.

VOICE. She's joined the herbal underground.

VOICE. Found herself a midwife.

VOICE. How thoroughly disgusting.

VOICE. She's refused amniocentesis, sonogram, psychosynthesis, DNA analysis, genetic counseling, growth hormone.

VOICE. Why didn't someone grab her and make her take the tests?

VOICE. This is still a free country.

VOICE. Of course, a technocracy.

[Theodora walks dreamily out the double doors into the arms of the doctors.]

VOICE. At what age can the fetus bring suit?

[Theodora Forensic appears at a lab door. She is wheeling a chair on which sits the talking head of Edward Chreode, her newborn, bodiless child. He is babbling uncontrollably as his head rolls, egg-like, on the seat. Theodora dotes on him, arranging his cap and the blankets around his neck as he talks.]

EDWARD CHREODE AS THE TALKING HEAD. Just like Sam Beckett, I retain a vivid memory of my mother's womb. I was carried, I said, with my head outside the universe. The body inside, inside of her, that one there who pushes my chair. But the head floated free in a space unexplored, a space denied, the space beyond space. Outside the universe, my head through a black hole in the firmament, I saw and I contemplated all. It occurred to me, free-floating in space, my head through a medium-sized black hole in the universe, that there is a transcendent cause, that some vast intelligence rules and we are the creatures of what this great thinking pulse is. I saw. There I saw. No surprises, no. Nothing new. Nothing to tell. Nothing to tell, because there is no one to hear. No one to listen to me. No hearers. Nothing heard from the head that once floated free from beyond the beyond. And suddenly saw the divine cause, the implicate order, rising in waves, and felt, yes, felt through the tremors in the iris of the eye, free floating the past being present, wave after wave of form giving form. The future attracting the past, pulling the past after it. The future desiring itself, attracting, pulling at form. And I being formed by everyone unusual who had ever lived, a talking head come from beyond, a bearer to earth of forms about to be lost. And I felt myself into each one. Yes, with my eyes, with my tongue, tasted, drank in, licked up, was part, devoured all previous shapes.

[*Theodora drops a cloth over his head. He is silent.*]

THEODORA. [*To the scientists, shadows on the wall*] I've brought you my child. As my rightful fathers, I wanted you to see what I've conceived.

[*She removes the cloth. He beings speaking immediately again.*]

TALKING HEAD. It's highly probable that beyond the beyond there is new beginning. If we ask ourselves where did the ability to generate form first arise, we have to remember that outside the universe is something else. Something like pure feeling. Yes, I said the word. Kill me. Kill me if you wish. Before I say something worse. Wave after wave of essence of creative capacity flows in the flesh, rises in us from beyond . . .

[*She drops the cloth again, he is silent.*]

[*All the Scientists point at Theodora screaming.*]

VOICES. Treason. Guilty of treason. Treasonous refusal to remove defective child from the womb. Now society suffers from gibberish. Guilty. Guilty. Sterilize her. Tie her down. Life unworthy of life cannot be allowed.

[*As the shadows rush towards Theodora, she manages to unveil the head once more. Philbert Wallace rushes out, dressed in surgical attire, rubber gloves. He drags Theodora Forensic out to be sterilized. As she is violated, Edward Chreode, immobile in the chair, keeps talking.*]

TALKING HEAD. There is sense to the universe, a thinking mind of creation, an incessant becoming, which we are bidden to know, out of which all form arises, rearranges, returning, resurfacing, there is meaning and most of all there is feeling. This knowledge, my friends, of oneness, and unity, of all things connected, this knowledge of infinite grace, organic compassion, ceaseless becoming, purpose, unfolding meaning, is the end result toward which science struggles . . .

[*A totally masked and gowned figure appears, drops the cloth over Edward's head. Silence. Wheels him out the double doors.*]

VOICE. Look at what we've done to Theodora Forensic.

VOICE. We could unblock her tubes.

VOICE. Let's make her new ones. From plastic.

VOICE. Plastic, of course. Plastic is wonderful.

VOICE. Let's rebuild Theodora Forensic.

VOICE. She must know the joys of motherhood.

VOICE. Yes, operate.

VOICE. What about him?

VOICE. Forget him. Put him away. Lock him up.

VOICE. Cut off his head.

VOICE. Cut off his head? Ha, ha, ha. [*Gales of laughter and Theodora wakes up.*]

DREAM ENDS.

THEODORA. I have to marry Philbert. Let him take my eggs, if he wants them. I've got to figure out gene alteration and transplant techniques.

SCENE 6

[*Theodora Forensic enters Edward Chreode's lab.*]

THEODORA. Edward Chreode, Philbert asked me to share these results.

EDWARD. Just a minute, Theodora, stay where you are. I have to clear something away. Rendezvous.

THEODORA. Oh, let me in, Edward. What have you got to hide?

EDWARD. Nothing. Rendezvous. Nothing at all.

THEODORA. Everyone knows about your big contract from the DOD.

EDWARD. Don't touch that. Don't sit over there. Rendezvous.

THEODORA. Why do you keep saying that word?

EDWARD. All right, Theodora. Sit down. I do have something that should interest you.

[*He turns on a projector. Various slides of the DNA are projected on the wall.*]

THEODORA. Edward, how absolutely beautiful it is. I'm always struck by the beauty of the genes. When I see someone small-minded or mean, I can't help but think, "but inside you are as beautiful as the Grand Canyon, or a tropical island, if you only knew."

EDWARD. It's the cancer gene spliced next to the gene for cardiovascular failure.

THEODORA. There does seem to be a distinct predilection to be weak one way or the other.

EDWARD. Rendezvous. Because of my work a pre-natal test is about to be marketed which will determine the likelihood of each unborn succumbing at some time in the future to either cancer or heart failure as well as the probable date of death from either illness. Then parents can decide, if the fetus shows a marked predilection for, say, childhood leukemia, or heart attack during peak earning years, whether or not they wish to terminate the pregnancy. And try again. Funny, how I've been led quite naturally from ideas about imminent extinction. Rendezvous. To this work on diseaseless perfection. Life insurance companies are already suing to gain access to longevity information.

So are the best colleges who don't see any reason to educate anyone but the fittest. I'm suddenly so busy with a whole range of experiments, and with all the graduate students I have to supervise. Rendezvous. I have no time to spend hours, as I used to, dreaming or speculating. But, then again, the days of creating science from dreams are gone. Now that the basic laws of nature are known, it's become a matter of filling in details, fitting together the pieces, developing technologies, securing a patent, marketing products. What a great time to be a biologist.

THEODORA. By the way, Edward, congratulations on your promotion.

EDWARD. Thank you. Rendezvous. Congratulations on your new laboratory and on your marriage.

THEODORA. Why do you keep saying that word?

EDWARD. Isn't it strange. It began in my sleep last night. I sat up straight and woke Mother with a shout. "Rendezvous," she told me at breakfast I screamed. Frankly, I can't even seem to tell when I say the word. Rendezvous.

THEODORA. Rendezvous. It's a meeting. Do you have an important meeting? But it also means surrender. "I surrender to you." "I put myself in your hands." "I give over to you." It's strange.

EDWARD. It's a small involuntary act, like a hiccup, perhaps.

THEODORA. But with meaning? Doesn't it make you stop to consider what you must have dreamed?

EDWARD. These days, I don't remember my dreams.

THEODORA. Oh, I never have. Certainly not since graduate school.

EDWARD. We're wasting time.

THEODORA. Yes, let's go on.

EDWARD. There's something quite tricky that we've begun to think about here in this laboratory. I tell you as a trusted colleague. Don't breathe a word. Could we not somehow shoot these genes into people who are not carrying them at all? Advancing armies, perhaps, suddenly decimated by fast-growing cancers or heart attacks? "Rendezvous." Then, if we could do away with these two major killers, our side would be left, basically, invulnerable. A defensive weapon with this potential might end the last possible threat of nuclear war and actually lead to disarmament. So that the field of molecular biology might actually right the great shame of physics. Then, we, on our side, would be left with the problems of aging. Might we not learn how to keep all the cells young for as long as the body functions? Then, perhaps, in cases of exceptional achievement, we could keep certain outstanding individuals alive for several hundred years or more. That sort of thing. Think how society would benefit. Rendezvous.

THEODORA. The only cells known to have the capacity for endless division are those which are malignant. It seems clear, we have to steal the secret of immortality from the cancerous cells and give it to the healthy cells which, at present, all die in good time.

EDWARD. Rendezvous. Rendezvous. Rendezvous!

THEODORA. Edward, are you in control of what you are saying?

EDWARD. Absolutely. Rendezvous. Between us we seem to be sitting on most far-reaching basic research discoveries in the realm of rendezvous. I do wish I could stop saying that rendezvous.

[*Edward Chreode is increasingly possessed by the word Rendezvous; his body is contorted with the effort of saying or not saying the word.*]

THEODORA. Have you noticed, Edward, the change in your usage? A minute ago, you were saying rendezvous as a sort of exclamation, but just now you've begun to use it within sentences itself, as if it had distinct meanings.

EDWARD. Rendezvous. To you, Theodora Forensic. Rendezvous. What can you possibly. Rendezvous. Of Rendezvous.

THEODORA. Edward, do you suppose you should see a neurologist? Dr. Leaderman down the hall is the best in his field.

[*The usually mild-mannered Edward Chreode chases Theodora Forensic out of his lab.*]

EDWARD. That son of a Rendezvous. Rendezvous. Is a butcher. I'll be Rendezvous. Momentarily. Don't Rendezvous. A word of this to anyone, especially not to my own Rendezvous. Or your Rendezvous. Himself. It would drive them both Rendezvous. Theodora, Rendezvous. Out of here. Do what I Rendezvous. Of you!

[*Alone, he tried desperately to steady himself.*]

EDWARD. Now, I must get a grip on my. Rendezvous.

[*Now a rather whimsical and improbable Beast appears at the door.*

The Beast is black and brown and short-haired with a hump on her back and the hump is covered with long, shaggy, darker hair. It has horns and large, round, expressive dark eyes. The Beast walks right up to Edward Chreode. Looks him straight in the eyes and clearly and distinctly says:]

BEAST. Rendezvous.

[*Edward Chreode faints.*]

[*The Beast begins to lick Edward Chreode, with a sloppy wet tongue, and to nuzzle him awake. Edward Chreode sits. The Beast, who has the sweetest of all imaginable voices, says:*]

BEAST. Rendezvous. Rendezvous.

EDWARD. Rendezvous.

BEAST. Rendezvous. Rendezvous.

EDWARD. Rendezvous.

[*The Beast nudges Edward Chreode up on his feet.*]

BEAST. Rendezvous Rendezvous.

[*Edward Chreode understands the invitation to dance. Edward Chreode and the Beast begin to dance to the beat of Rendezvous. They make music with the word and with little bells, and they dance to the beat of the Rendezvous song. When the dance is done, Edward Chreode embraces the Beast, who lays her head on Chreode's shoulders. They speak to one another, pledging eternal fidelity, using the one word of their common language.*]

BEAST. [*Now, I must go. Don't forget me.*] Rendezvous. Rendezvous. Rendezvous.

EDWARD. (*Don't leave me. Don't go.*] Rendezvous. Rendezvous. Rendezvous.

BEAST. [*I must go. Don't forget me.*] Rendezvous. Rendezvous. Rendezvous.

EDWARD. [*I will never forget you.*] Rendezvous.

[*The Beast goes out the door, nearly running into Haila in her wheelchair, who does not notice. The Beast steps aside, letting her enter, and throws one long look at Edward Chreode before vanishing. Edward, visibly unsettled, nevertheless attempts to appear calm before his mother.*]

HAILA. Edward, you've frightened that poor girl half to death. I want you to speak to me now without once using that word.

EDWARD. Certainly, mother. No cause for excitement. I'm fine. Never felt better.

HAILA. Bad dreams have no place in a lab.

EDWARD. Mother, I'm fully recovered.

HAILA. Very good, Edward. We'll forget this unfortunate lapse ever happened. As you continue to advance, Edward, you'll learn that forgetfulness is a great virtue. It's impossible to live a productive life without forgetting a good deal of what happens to oneself. Now, duty calls us both.

EDWARD. Of course, Mother, back to work.

HAILA. Yes, yes. My research has taken a particularly difficult turn. I'm all alone, without a close colleague, partner, or husband. No, I've never had a true companion in work. Never an equal to comfort or inspire or pay the bills. And memory, Edward — this fact of being able to recall what is past — has plagued me all my life. Why shouldn't the past simply cease to exist? It could, if the evolutionary information were contained completely in genes. The present would be enough. Why, then, does the flesh need to hold on?

[*Haila wheels herself out. The Beast sticks her head around the door.*]

BEAST. Rendezvous.

[*Edward Chreode, his head turned away from the Beast, shakes his entire body in an attitude of despair and dismay at what has happened/ is happening to him.*]

INTERMISSION

SCENE 7

[*Absolutely deafening applause.*]

[*Triumphal music, celebratory lights. Theodora wheels Haila backwards in front of the stage. Haila throws confetti at Philbert Wallace who is carried in on the shoulders of Edward Chreode and another scientist in white lab coat. Philbert is deposited on stage at the podium. This is Philbert's* DREAM. *He begins to speak.*]

PHILBERT. Today, I'm thrilled to announce to the entire human race that we have completely mastered gene alteration techniques. There are no defects we cannot correct.

THEODORA. He's brilliant. Absolutely brilliant. What a mind. How glad I am to join my genes with his.

HAILA. I'm prouder of him than I am of my own flesh and blood. I consider him my real son.

EDWARD. What a man! The best around. I am honored to assist in his great plans.

PHILBERT. Suffering has been abolished by us, the genetic scientists. No loss, no pain, no doubt, no handicaps, mental or emotional, come between the individual and his or her full potential. Everyone is optimized at genius level.

[*Thunderous applause.*]

HAILA. At last, we are freed from destiny and fate. Freed from the past.

PHILBERT. Of course, we must now leave the earth which threatens us still with disease and with death. The entire galaxy beckons us, offering unparalleled potential for economic development and human betterment.

[*Thunderous applause. Philbert holds up his hands for silence.*]

Ladies and gentlemen, I have a special surprise guest for you this afternoon. May I have your attention and a very warm welcome for our very own Mother Earth.

[In Philbert's dream, Haila is Mother Earth. She comes to the podium wearing a plastic world globe which is decorated to look like a rather frowsy suburban matron's hat. She speaks in a halting, low, apologetic, passive, mother's voice.]

THE EARTH. Thank you, Philbert. Thank you very much. Well, I thought . . . I'm not really used to public speaking. I hardly ever say anything at all. But I thought, well, as you are all about to depart, well, I couldn't really let you go without offering some few words of advice. You know how mothers are. We always do want the best for our children and we try, well, we do try, in our own imperfect ways, to do the right thing. We worry, you know. Those of you who are mothers will understand what I mean. Are there any mothers left out there? Oh, yes, yes, I see a few hands, one or two.

Yes, well then, you will understand. You will understand what I mean when I say one of the hardest things to do is to admit the mistakes you've made with your children. To really look hard at your own failings and at all the ways your own limitations have warped your offspring.

Yes, well, all we mothers can do is try. We all do try just as hard as we can. Now, of course, that you've perfected birth, you've forgotten all of that. No one woman is responsible. Perhaps I should have thought it out like that. Maybe it's the best way, after all. In any case I wish you luck. And I do just want to take a moment of your time to leave you all with a few parting words. Some little saying to carry away, some words to live by on your outer-spatial journey. Well, I'm not going to tell you how much I'm going to miss you. I will miss you. That might seem strange to you, after all the troubles we've had, but I will miss you. I know you don't think you're going to miss me one little bit, but I have always had your best interests at heart. I have tried and I have given a lot. I've done my best. And if that best wasn't good enough, well, now, I promised myself I wouldn't go on like this. I really just came here because I do simply want to leave you all with a word or two that might somehow be helpful. I'll try not to bore you with much, but I did want to say, well, in all these years that you've been here with me, and in the all the years before you came, and maybe, too, in all the years to come once you leave me alone to clean up your mess, I've only had one thought, really, one thought only has guided me. Odd, how hard it is to put it into words. I suppose I had hoped you would see it for yourselves.

Well, all right, now. Yes. Yes. Let me tell you that one thought of mine I always have had. It goes a little bit like this: No matter what ever happened, no matter how many mistakes I made, no matter what ever was done to me, from the first time they cut me to mine oil and coal, to the time they dropped the atom bomb, to more recent years when they took from me the secrets of the genes and started putting human growth hormones into pigs so the poor little things couldn't stand up, and were depressed all the time, I've always thought only one thing, and it's been this: Whatever happens to you, Mother, you just keep on doing what you've always done, you just keep on answering everything with life, you just keep putting forth life, you just keep making the green earth sprout. And in the cities, you know, I had the plants grow right up through the sidewalks. And even in the barren deserts and the jungles I made so many diverse species. Why the colors on the wings of the moths alone, well, I thought that would give you pause. I really thought you would understand. Well, that's all I wanted to say. I just wanted to remind you and ask you to remember that as you go on your way. It wasn't enough, I understand. It wasn't enough to make you happy in the end. Maybe in space where there aren't any other forms of life you will be more comfortable and you'll be able to look after yourselves better out there than you have done here, where you had so many brothers and sisters and the competition seemed to overwhelm you. So I wish the very best to each and every human being. Thank you for taking the time to listen to me. Thank you, Philbert. Thank you all.

[*Silence.*]

PHILBERT. Thank you, Mother. How about a round of applause!

DREAM ENDS

[*Theodora enters, holding print-out material.*]

THEODORA. Philbert, I must speak with you.

PHILBERT. [*Snaps awake, takes her pages, scans them hastily.*] Theodora, I find these results unsatisfactory.

THEODORA. So do I, of course — that's why I'm here.

PHILBERT. These results are inconclusive. We need the answer. We need a foolproof method for gene alteration. We need it now.

THEODORA. But it isn't going to work.

[*She storms out. He follows her through the hall to her office.*]

PHILBERT. Of course it will work.

THEODORA. Look, Philbert, we've already proven conclusively that the attachment of new genetic material has completely unpredictable effects. The organism becomes confused. It seems to me that DNA has been vastly overrated.

PHILBERT. Theodora, do you want a divorce?

THEODORA. Yes.

PHILBERT. Traitor.

THEODORA. I can't make gene alteration work.

PHILBERT. You were my brightest hope, Theodora, the brilliant star on the horizon. You've failed me, Theodora. My lawyer will phone your lawyer in the morning.

THEODORA. Philbert, something we haven't dreamed of yet is happening.

PHILBERT. Legally, I'm entitled to joint custody of your eggs and if you don't behave admirably, I'll sue you for full custody in perpetuity.

THEODORA. I'm telling you I have to abandon all my research. What do you think I am, a prize-winning hen?

PHILBERT. Teamwork, Theodora, teamwork. Your eggs and my sperm.

THEODORA. I don't need to reproduce, Philbert. I need to work.

PHILBERT. My parents didn't care what I achieved, Theodora. They had no aspirations for their son. My father was a mechanic; my mother cooked lunches at the high school. As a child, I used to dream that these people were just my surrogate caregivers, and that my real parents, my gene donors, were out in the real world, brilliantly successful, rich. Maybe I was right. Legally, Theodora, I am owed your eggs.

THEODORA. Take my eggs, Philbert, if you want them so much.

PHILBERT. You really are totally without maternal feeling.

THEODORA. I suppose I can stand one thoroughly invasive medical procedure. The pain might be a relief from the unbearable agony of this failed research.

PHILBERT. For a real woman, the pain is bearable. We simply drill a small hole through the uterine wall.

THEODORA. I know the procedure, Philbert.

PHILBERT. Give me your eggs, Theodora, I'll forget I ever wanted you to share my life.

THEODORA. Maybe I'm not as brilliant as you had hoped, Philbert? Did you ever consider that? Maybe my eggs aren't worth much. Maybe I'm a fraud.

PHILBERT. Nonsense. I'll take care of your eggs, Theodora. I'll see to the details of their fertilization and their implantation. I'll follow through on their maturation. I'll send them to all the great universities. I'll let you remain a fully funded researcher in my lab.

THEODORA. I tell you, I'm stuck. I don't know which way to turn.

PHILBERT. How many short-sighted people said the atom couldn't be split. Genes can be altered. They will be. We will do it. Here, in these labs. All of us. Together. Like a family, Theodora. We must. Theodora, I want you standing next to me the day we conquer DNA. We can reconsider our divorce, Theodora. It was never just for your eggs . . . I had hoped . . .

THEODORA. No, Philbert, no. These personal things mean nothing to me. You're right, of course — I can't start questioning the very premises of all of our work just because I'm momentarily frustrated.

PHILBERT. Think! Theodora, think!

THEODORA. Maybe if I can devise a simple alteration in the experimental technique, perhaps if I change the order of several steps . . . yes, I begin to see a way to proceed. Let me take another look at those results.

PHILBERT. That's the spirit, Theodora. I'll schedule you in for complete egg removal.

THEODORA. [*Thoroughly preoccupied*] Right, Philbert, right. Just make certain they don't want to keep me overnight. I can't take that much time off.

[*She takes the papers and leaves.*]

SCENE 8

[Edward Chreode enters his lab, goes to the blackboard, begins to draw some figures, steps back speculative. The Beast enters quietly. Sees him. Hides herself behind him. He sees the open door. Shuts it, somewhat dismayed. Returns to work. He backs up. The Beast bites his rump. He jumps.]

EDWARD. You're back! I hope no one saw you come in. This is a high-security floor.

[Edward Chreode impulsively hugs the Beast.]

EDWARD. You're the last of your species, your kind. You needed water and trees; you needed wetland and sun. You must be lonely as hell. That's where I come in — me, Chreode, your friend the geneticist. That's why you found your way here. I understand. Instinct. Incredible. Absolutely astonishing.

[The Beast begins to circle, looking for a place to lie down.]

EDWARD. Make yourself at home. Yes, yes. That's right. I suppose I should sit, shouldn't I? Sit here? With you?

[Edward Chreode sits next to the Beast.]

EDWARD. Ever since our first rendezvous, I've been thinking about what to do.

[The Beast stretches out, rolls over, clearly wanting to be scratched.]

EDWARD. Oh, well, all right. Is this what you want? You like that? Yes, yes, pishky-pisk, minsky-bisk.

[He nuzzles the Beast. They play for awhile. Edward Chreode grows quite animal-like for a moment, then abruptly snaps back to human form. He becomes quite doctor-like.]

EDWARD. I've been thinking quite hard. If we were to take a few of your eggs . . . go in and grab what we can. With the eggs in a dish, there's a chance I could stimulate them to clone. Or, if cloning didn't work, I could fertilize your eggs with something else. A bull or rhinoceros, say — the choices are many. I'd put the eggs back into you. You could have a natural birth. Or, rather, more likely, a Cesarean section, in most IVF treatments the risk ends up being too great for vaginal delivery. Forgive me for sounding so intimate. You could have triplets, or quints. They'd be so cute. We hope. Transgenic species have a very high incidence of birth defect. But let's not dwell on the negative. If you'd rather not bother about any of this, we'd implant your fertilized eggs into some cows. Cows are plentiful and docile. They could bring your offspring to term. Your little ones would live in all the best zoos.

[*The Beast shakes her head "no."*]

EDWARD. No? Did you shake your head "no?"

[*The Beast shakes her head "yes."*]

EDWARD. That's better, of course. "Yes," yes is the response we want.

[*The Beast shakes her head again, "no."*]

EDWARD. But why not? Why on earth not? It's worth a try. A try after all. You have no right to become extinct.

[*He has come very close to her. He is speaking most intimately. The Beast opens her mouth wide. Makes a siren sound.*]

EDWARD. What a very large mouth. With so many teeth.

[*The Beast makes the sound again.*]

EDWARD. What an alarm. What a shout.

[*Edward Chreode is drawn into the mouth of the beast. She begins to gulp him down.*]

EDWARD. [*From inside the beast*] But you're eating me up. Please stop. I beg of you, stop.

[*The Beast's belly stretches open, as the Beast moves forward gulping Chreode. Through transparent gauze we see Edward inside her belly.*]

EDWARD. Why would you do such a thing? It's warm in here. Not too warm. No. Comfortable. Fine. Warm and light. There's a glow. What a beautiful sight. You are splendid inside. Someone's coming this way. Who could it be?

THEODORA. [*Also inside the beast. Distraught.*] Lost, lost everything lost. Everything taken away.

EDWARD. Theodora? Theodora Forensic! What in the world are you doing here?

THEODORA. All is lost. Lost.

EDWARD. Theodora, I'm here. It's Edward. Edward Chreode. Can you float towards me? A little to the left.

THEODORA. Float. Yes. Float. I'm so light. A brain. A brain floating in space. A brain cut from a heart.

EDWARD. Theodora, can you grab my hand as you float by? Here we are, floating free.

THEODORA. My eggs, my eggs, where did they put them? Are they hatched somewhere else? My ducks, my little chicks.

EDWARD. Theodora, it's Edward, Edward Chreode. You must have been swallowed just as I was.

THEODORA. This place, this place isn't right. I'm empty inside.

EDWARD. Theodora . . .

THEODORA. I was born in a dish. I go stiff whenever I'm touched. Where did I put them? I need to gather them up. I never knew flesh. I must find them.

EDWARD. Theodora, you're breaking my heart. We are cradled in light, don't you see? Rest here with me.

THEODORA. No rest. No. I must look. I must search. I must find them. Count them all. Put them back.

EDWARD. Theodora, wait, don't float away. Don't despair. How lost she seems. How deranged.

How alive I suddenly feel. Even her sadness rushes through me. How new I've become. Fully ensouled, if I might say it like that. Yes, full of soul. The world soul, if I might use such a phrase. It passes through me like breath. I'm trembling. Trembling with powerful feelings. I'm so full. So very full. The light is so bright. It's growing hot all around. I'm at the center. Touching the core. I'm plummeting down. I'm lofting. I'm touching the heart. I'm going up. I'm flying, I'm, I'm letting go, shattering, breaking apart. Fractured. Fragmented. Blown up. Exploded. I'm exhausted. How tender I feel.

[*Haila wheels in.*]

HAILA. Edward! Edward?

[*Philbert races in. The Beast is right there, but they don't see her.*]

PHILBERT. Chreode, take a look at this . . .

HAILA. He's not answering me.

PHILBERT. Chreode, goddamned man . . . Has he gone home already? It's only eight o'clock.

HAILA. Not without me.

PHILBERT. I need him.

HAILA. I need him, too. And don't forget, I made him by myself.

[She stands as she speaks, as if transported out of herself by a vision all her own. Philbert neither hears nor sees; he is too bound to a mechanistic world in which such events don't happen.]

HAILA. I was alone when I pushed him out with a great triumphal shout. I made him at great risk. Carried him in secret. Birthed him alone on the run in a field. Birds sang. I nursed him at my breast. I felt the pull of his little mouth. The war seemed far away. Now I understand. The body tunes in when the proper time comes.

[She pauses, sits slowly down.]

HAILA. What in the world does that mean?

PHILBERT. Who knows, Haila? What do you mean ever?

[Philbert begins to wheel her out.]

PHILBERT. Come on. I'll put you in a cab. The Prize Committee meets next week. I need your results. Don't screw me up.

EDWARD. That was close. Odd, but I felt not the slightest urge to respond. Once you've been, well, floated like this, completely protected, met, accepted, and touched, drenched in such sweetness, you're never the same.

[Edward begins to emerge, head first, from the Beast's mouth. He comes out in fetal position. Having "died," he is "reborn."]

[The Beast gives an exhausted sigh.]

EDWARD. Yes, my goodness, what a labor you've made.

[The Beast gets up. Edward helps.]

You've totally changed me. I had a vision so complete.

[The Beast makes a sound.]

[Edward Chreode embraces the Beast.]

EDWARD. How did it ever come to this? Extinct. I can't stand it. I must remember it all. I must not let this feeling leave my flesh. We must work, you and I, to understand it. We must describe what we know. Write a book. The first cross species collaboration.

[*The Beast casts a wide-eyed look out in the audience's direction and rolls her eyes.*]

You must help me, by your presence, your breath, your deep and mysterious eyes, gateways they are, to your . . .

[*The phone rings.*]

[*Edward picks it up. During his conversation, the Beast ambles out.*]

Philbert, it's you. Yes. Yes, the results. They're on my desk. Not yet written up. Yes, right away. Well, I've been busy. I've been involved. With work, Philbert. With theories, with thoughts. [*He listens.*] Well since you put it like that I have something to say to you, too. It's like this . . . it's well . . . it's just that . . . I'm through. Yes, that sounds right. I'm through, Philbert! I'm done. I've had it. I quit. I resign. I tender my resignation. I'm into something new. I'm finished with the DOD. I'm done with your damned genetic manipulations, your pseudo-scientific reproductive "ethics." Go fuck yourself in a dish.

[*Philbert enters in the middle of the speech.*]

PHILBERT. Edward, Edward, I know. I understand. The work is so hard, so difficult.

EDWARD. I mean it, Philbert. I mean what I say. I'm leaving the lab, the war work.

PHILBERT. Defense work . . . for God's sake . . .

EDWARD. I'm done with your search for a super race, disease-free and perfect, forget it! Altering genes! It's arrogant. Repulsive.

PHILBERT. Edward, Edward, the words you use! Calm down. Take a few days . . . go out to my cottage at the lake. Let nature renew you.

EDWARD. Nature. What do you know about nature? How dare you mention nature to me!

PHILBERT. Look, I've had a rough week myself. Personal things get in the way of research.

EDWARD. Personal things? Like what? Owning genes? You're an imperialist, Philbert, that's what you are. A colonialist. Colonizing proteins in a dish.

PHILBERT. Edward, calm down. You're not making sense.

EDWARD. How could I expect you to understand? I need time to do my own work.

PHILBERT. Your own work?

EDWARD. DNA has been overrated. Something else altogether may be happening. Gene alteration isn't even interesting.

PHILBERT. Really?

EDWARD. Philbert, think along with me for a moment. Each cell has the same genetic make-up, but some cells form hands, others feet or skin or brain. Right?

PHILBERT. Right.

EDWARD. Genes are certainly not the sole determinants of traits or of forms. Something else is at work, but what?

PHILBERT. What, indeed, Edward, what? It's the great unsolved question of biology.

EDWARD. A memory . . . could that really be it? . . . of past forms lodged in energy fields that exist outside the organism but speak to it. It sounds mad, and yet . . . I feel it. The laws of nature might not be fixed for all time. They might evolve. The life force, Philbert, is real.

PHILBERT. I feel sorry for you. You never made it. Now you're spouting some sort of pseudo-religious prattle. Face it, Chreode, you're a failure.

EDWARD. You've become myopic staring at those computer printouts. I intend to offer a new paradigm. A new way of seeing. Creativity is within nature, Philbert. Nature's laws are not fixed. Change, creativity, is life.

PHILBERT. That's philosophy. That's metaphysics . . .

EDWARD. All science is metaphysics . . .

PHILBERT. That's bullshit . . .

EDWARD. We ought to participate, Philbert, with fate. It's taken the universe billions of years to create.

PHILBERT. Fuck fate!

EDWARD. Don't you see, my ideas point towards a whole new science of life.

PHILBERT. You're a third rate, washed-up, uninspired scientist.

EDWARD. We can't any longer ignore the possibility that creativity is real. Everything may not be given in advance. New patterns of organization may be made up as the world goes on.

PHILBERT. You're a weirdo, a fanatic, Edward, not a scientist.

EDWARD. Nature is creative. Alive. The laws of nature evolve. I feel certain about that. The details need working out.

PHILBERT. Nature this. Nature that. As if nature was anything but a mess. A mass murderer through hurricane, earthquake, flood, drought . . . and what about plain old death!

EDWARD. Philbert, please. I'm trying to think. I can't deal with your death anxiety now, though that's what is driving you to try to control everything.

PHILBERT. You're a megalomaniac with paranoid tendencies and delusions of grandeur. Someday we'll be able to diagnose your kind in the dish and flush you down the sink.

EDWARD. Science needs heretics, Philbert.

PHILBERT. You're the dotty associate professor we have to store in a closet. Got tenure because your *mother* works here.

EDWARD. No, Philbert, I intend to research, to write, publish, speak out. But first, I've got to clean up this lab. Get some plants. Find the right staff.

PHILBERT. Just remember, you're not going to get one dime. Each time you open your mouth, you'll be laughed right out of the scientific discourse. Edward, you've just deconstructed yourself!

[*Philbert exits. Chreode exits double doors. He is liberated.*]

SCENE 9

[Theodora is asleep in her laboratory. Philbert enters, carrying an infant in his arms.]

PHILBERT. Wake up. Look at this.

[She takes the blanket, unwraps it, looks.]

THEODORA. It's one of ours.

PHILBERT. Yes, Theodora.

THEODORA. Pale.

PHILBERT. Duchenne's muscular dystrophy. Despite every precautionary test. Plus, massive childhood heart dysfunction.

THEODORA. Poor little thing. Does it have a name?

PHILBERT. Unforeseen mutation in the carrier woman's womb. Due perhaps to drug residue from artificial stimulation of your ovum.

THEODORA. It oughtn't to die unnamed, do you think?

PHILBERT. Strange events still occur in utero, outside our scrutiny or control.

THEODORA. Justin. Let's call him that. It's a sweet name for a boy. Don't you think?

PHILBERT. Gene therapy is urgent. Necessary. Tests show his intellectual potential is at genius level.

THEODORA. Poor little one. Mama loves you. Loves you anyhow.

PHILBERT. Your license to begin gene therapy in humans came through this morning. You are the world leader in gene therapy. Congratulations, Theodora.

THEODORA. All my work to date has been on terminally ill patients.

PHILBERT. This child will die without massive intervention, now.

THEODORA. And the side effects have been positively frightening.

PHILBERT. Save our child, Theodora.

THEODORA. He has your eyes, Philbert. How sweet to see your eyes without that glinty look.

PHILBERT. Operate.

THEODORA. I don't know enough.

PHILBERT. Risk!

THEODORA. What beautiful hands. He has the hands of a surgeon.

PHILBERT. I have a team of the best surgeons standing by. There isn't any time. The press are on alert. The videos ready to roll.

[*They are drawn together, admiring the child.*]

THEODORA. Oh, Philbert, it's awful. It's breaking my heart.

PHILBERT. I know. I know.

THEODORA. Oh, Justin, listen now to what I say. You needn't be afraid. I'll be with you the entire time. I'll sit and rock you.

PHILBERT. Distance yourself, for God's sake. You were just the egg donor.

THEODORA. An experimental lamb, that's all he is.

PHILBERT. Think, Theodora, think!

THEODORA. Will you put on some Bach?

PHILBERT. Of course, if it will help you think.

THEODORA. Turn off the bright lights.

[*Philbert turns off the lights, switches on music. Mozart begins to play.*]

THEODORA. Mozart, better yet, a genius dying young, wildly proud, ecstatic, brave.

PHILBERT. Give me back that child.

THEODORA. I need a rocking chair.

PHILBERT. Give me back my son.

THEODORA. I believe in a dignified death, Philbert.

PHILBERT. Make him well!

THEODORA. He shouldn't have to suffer anymore.

PHILBERT. Fix him.

THEODORA. I don't know enough.

[*Philbert grabs her, furious, upset.*]

PHILBERT. Pull yourself together.

[*Theodora runs from him, sheltering the child.*]

THEODORA. Leave us alone.

[*Philbert goes after her. Grabs her again.*]

PHILBERT. Save my son!

THEODORA. Philbert, let us be.

PHILBERT. Operate!

THEODORA. I can't.

PHILBERT. Transplant!

THEODORA. I won't.

PHILBERT. Coward!

THEODORA. Get out!

PHILBERT. Murderer!

[*In a rage, Philbert grabs her and rips the child from her arms. In the struggle the "baby" falls to the ground. Philbert exits. The sound of shattering glass. Theodora wakes from her dream to find she has knocked over a laboratory beaker. She kneels and begins to pick up the broken pieces.*]

THEODORA. Oh, shit, I'm so clumsy.

[*Philbert enters Theodora's lab.*]

PHILBERT. Theodora, I've got great news. Here, here, what have you done?

[*They kneel on the floor together, picking up the broken glass.*]

PHILBERT. Theodora, your license just came through from the RAC. You are the first geneticist granted permission to perform gene alteration experiments on non-terminally ill patients.

THEODORA. I know, Philbert, I know.

PHILBERT. What do you mean, you know? I just got the call. We'll go out. Celebrate. Talk through the details. Plan the press conference. We've done it, Theodora. The future's ours.

[*Impulsively, he hugs her. Upon contact, they both go suddenly stiff in one another's arms.*]

THEODORA. Wait a minute, Philbert, wait a minute. I no longer believe in what I'm doing.

PHILBERT. Theodora, why, at every moment of impending

momentous success, do you sabotage yourself with doubt like this?

THEODORA. By themselves the genes don't know enough. And neither do I.

PHILBERT. We can do gene alterations, now. Gene transplants. We've been given the green light, Theodora. The go ahead. I can taste it. I can smell the success on my hands.

THEODORA. Not yet.

PHILBERT. But you know how to do it!

THEODORA. I don't want to implement that technology now.

[*Philbert, enraged and threatening, bears down on her.*]

PHILBERT. Have you gone mad? We've been mandated by the NIH to do gene alterations on human beings. The last snag has just passed the RAC. You've had privileges, Theodora, funding, esteem . . . now you have to deliver. You have to do what you're told . . .

[*Haila, wheeled by Edward, enters Theodora's lab, interrupting the fight. Philbert throws up his hands in total frustration. Edward, sensing the danger in the air, goes to stand next to Theodora.*]

HAILA. Good. Everyone is here. I have something very important to say.

[*Pause.*]

HAILA. I've decided to die today.

[*Edward and Theodora begin to move towards her.*]

HAILA. Don't protest. Don't try to stop me. My mind's made up. I don't need your help to die. I know exactly how. The knowledge comes from being fertile for so long. But before I die, I have a legacy to leave each one of you.

Therefore, I require your complete attention. Philbert, you are first, as you always do insist. Before I hand you this [*she holds up a paper*] let me give a brief synopsis of its contents. Memory is not stored within the brain. This, Philbert, is my last, great, astounding finding. Memory fields surround the world.

EDWARD. Mother, that's amazing.

HAILA. [*She ignores Edward.*] Philbert, I leave this paper as my legacy to you. It drives a coffin nail into your mechanistic view. Philbert, you are wrong. Your premises are false. Generecombo, Inc. is headed straight for bankruptcy. And you, Philbert, are headed for obscurity.

[*She hands Philbert the paper.*]

PHILBERT. Haila, Haila, ever since I came as an acolyte to your lab, I've waited in vain for one single word of praise from you. One word of true encouragement, one expression of pride in me, Haila, one pat on the back. And you've always denied me that.

[*Edward's curiosity about the contents of the paper is virtually uncontainable. Edward sneaks up behind Philbert, trying, in vain, to read the paper which Philbert dangles in his shaking hand.*]

PHILBERT. I wanted mother love from you, Haila. I wanted warmth, appreciation, a sense of family, of belonging. I wanted you to rejoice in my prowess, my knowledge, my work. You gave me science. You taught me reverence, perseverance. You taught me to play with my thoughts, to risk, to dream, to follow the wild hunch. Then you poisoned everything you taught. You warped my essence with your constant demands, your criticisms, your brutal need to compete with me at every turn, your endless tales of your woes, your cruel withholding of praise. You charmed me into serving you, you mocked me out loud to others, you tortured me with your put-downs, your rejections. You expected complete loyalty from me, complete subservience. You destroyed my core, my center. You made me feel you despised me for my emptiness. Why, Haila, couldn't you ever, for once, have stopped your infernal self-involvement long enough to see who I was?

[*Silence.*]

EDWARD. Why didn't you give *me* your paper?

PHILBERT. And, now, with your dying breath, you've betrayed me with this, Haila, this insignificant piece of work, this stupid, backward, romantic thesis of your dotage, this last feeble attempt at undermining everything I've ever stood for. Finally, I know how cruel and perverse you really are.

[*He begins to tear up the paper, and as he does, Edward dives for the pieces at his feet.*]

PHILBERT. You will not discredit me, Haila, you won't because I am correct. We are chemicals, nothing else. I am going to mastermind alteration of the genes. I'll do it alone, without any of you. Then, Haila, we'll all be perfect and free, free of disease, free of the poison of your baseless, senseless, cruel passions, your competitiveness, your lack of love.

[*The paper is in shreds on the floor. Edward begins to piece them back together. Philbert stands erect, back in icy control of himself as Haila delivers her final blow.*]

HAILA. That paper will be published tomorrow in *Science Magazine*. It kills your reductionistic view.

[*Edward stands; Philbert exits furiously.*]

HAILA. Theodora, come . . .

THEODORA. [*Completely shocked*] A disagreement, yes, but to ignore and destroy *data.*

HAILA. Philbert reacted exactly as I expected. I leave

him my life's work, a brilliant paper with extraordinary implications . . .

EDWARD. Revolutionary.

HAILA. He ignores and destroys my work as the entire male scientific establishment has always done. You see, Theodora, you are not safe as long as you have to depend upon the male establishment for funding, for prizes or prestige. They'll pick your brain. They'll always say women can't do science. In order for a woman to have a lasting impact, Theodora, you need independence! Money! A lab of your own! I'm leaving you my fortune, Theodora. I've scrimped and saved all my life. Recently, I received quite a handsome advance from Generecombo, Inc. I've got enough, Theodora, to leave you a handsomely equipped laboratory funded in perpetuity. I appoint you chief scientist of that lab and head of the Haila Gudenschmartzer Institute for the Advancement of Women's Truths in Science.

THEODORA. Oh, Haila, Haila . . . No one has ever . . .

HAILA. Stop blubbering. You've got your work cut out for you.

THEODORA. No one has ever trusted me; let me be myself, take my time.

HAILA. Stop wallowing in the past, Theodora. You're head of your own institute now. Give me a program.

THEODORA. I want to completely rethink the technology. I'm going back to a detailed study of embryology. I'm going to look at environmental and social causes of infertility, birth defect, illness of all sorts. I'm going to talk to pregnant women. Haila, with your money, I can do so many things.

HAILA. Daughter!

THEODORA. Mother!

[They embrace for a moment, then Haila, businesslike, pushes Theodora away. Haila takes a round chrome container from her lap. It smokes mysteriously.]

HAILA. Edward, I leave this box to you . . .

[Haila hands it to him.]

HAILA. Inside are all my eggs.

[Edward drops the box.]

EDWARD. What?

HAILA. Pick them up.

[He picks up the box.]

HAILA. Yes, Edward, inside that box are all my eggs. I had intended to put them in the Nobel Sperm Bank but that won't be possible now, as I won't win the prize. So I bequeath them to you, my son.

EDWARD. Your eggs? Whatever for? What can I do . . .

HAILA. Clone me. Make me new.

THEODORA. Oh, yes!

EDWARD. Clone you?

HAILA. Think what enormous benefit to humankind you would perform.

EDWARD. I couldn't do such a thing.

HAILA. With my dying breath, I bequeath my eggs to you.

EDWARD. *[He opens the box.]* Yes, there they are. Each and every one. My God.

HAILA. Make me as I might have been. Unsullied by oppression, history, or fate.

EDWARD. Whatever could that mean? Who would you be if you were cloned?

THEODORA. Oh, Edward, shut the lid. You'll ruin them in the air.

HAILA. Make me fresh.

EDWARD. What about the war? What about standing up to Hitler? What about the constant struggle with your work? Your disability? Your dreams? What about your heart? Your soul? Is all that chemical? Can it be made again? What about your giving birth to me?

[*Edward takes an egg in his hand and suddenly he eats it. He takes another, eats it.*]

THEODORA. Edward, stop.

EDWARD. I have to do it. What else can I do? Mother cloned. Without her particular passion, her hard-won self. Absurd! Actually, they taste quite good.

THEODORA. How dare you.

EDWARD. She entrusted them to me.

THEODORA. She asked to be cloned.

EDWARD. She understands the folly of that last request.

THEODORA. Haila? Haila? Oh, Edward, she's nearly dead and you're eating up her eggs. Stop.

EDWARD. At the end, she was on the right track. I feel it.

[*Edward takes another mouthful.*]

THEODORA. Oh, Haila, please, speak up.

HAILA. [*Reviving*] How predictable you are, each one. Chew, Edward, chew.

EDWARD. [*He takes her by the shoulders.*] Theodora, you keep on with your hard research. I'll continue my theoretical pursuits. We're right. I feel it. Together, we'll get onto something. Mother had begun to see it. A new understanding, a new participatory relationship with nature has to be articulated. The imaginative forces in the universe are key, inherent creativity. I'm beginning to have a sense of it. I feel it.

THEODORA. [*Still held by him, looking into his eyes*] Edward, I'm falling love with you. You have such passion, such great gentleness, such strength, such a strange, compelling vision . . . I love you . . . but I've given away my eggs.

EDWARD. Don't worry, Theodora. I love you for your mind, your heart, not for your reproductive parts. We'll adopt.

THEODORA. Edward!

EDWARD. Theodora!

THEODORA. Together, we'll do science.

[*They kiss.*]

THEODORA AND EDWARD. Yes, yes, yes.

HAILA. [*Revives*] Yes, I had it once, love. And you know who it was with? Henri Bergson. A great philosophic mind. As brilliant as I. On a beach. Underneath the sky. Animal-like. I was of his flesh. He of mine. I knew with my body. With my insides I thought. With him, I could have done anything, accomplished everything, been myself. Age came between us. History. Death. How could I have forgotten that? Blanked it out. It hurt too much. To have it once. Never again. To find and lose. The life of human beings is hard. Theodora, Edward, listen to me, I've decided to live awhile more. Memory is spirit, you see. Proof that the spirit exists.

Theodora, wheel me back to the lab. We have an institute to plan. Edward, back to work. Dream on! Speculate!

[Theodora wheels Haila out. Edward exits Theodora's lab. Immediately, he enters his own lab. Music begins, at first just the sound of waves. Contemplative, he decides to turn on the slide projector. He does, but instead of the projections he had intended, beautiful, intense close-ups of nature (flowers, insects, trees, animals) are projected all over the set. It's as if these images have come directly out of Chreode. He begins shedding his lab coat. He reaches out toward the images he sees. He is entering another state of consciousness. He takes off his shirt, his pants. He begins to assume the form of different animals in order to sense their particular animal selves. Sometimes he pauses, as if caught between his half-man/half-animal-self. As the projected nature images end, the walls of the laboratory begin to fall, section by section, until the laboratory has disappeared. The night sky is revealed. Stars rise all over. Music intensifies. Chreode becomes a praying mantis, a slithering snake, an insect-eating frog, and finally a lion eating Chreode's tie. Edward Chreode stretches out, listening. He is enveloped by nature, dappled by starlight. He waits. A Baby-Beast, covered in fur but with a bright human face, scampers in. She plays by herself, then goes to Chreode, licks him, plays with his toes. The Beast follows her baby. Baby-Beast and Beast lie down next to Chreode. Stars begin to dim. Out of the falling silence, the Baby-Beast's voice is heard: "Rendezvous."]

END

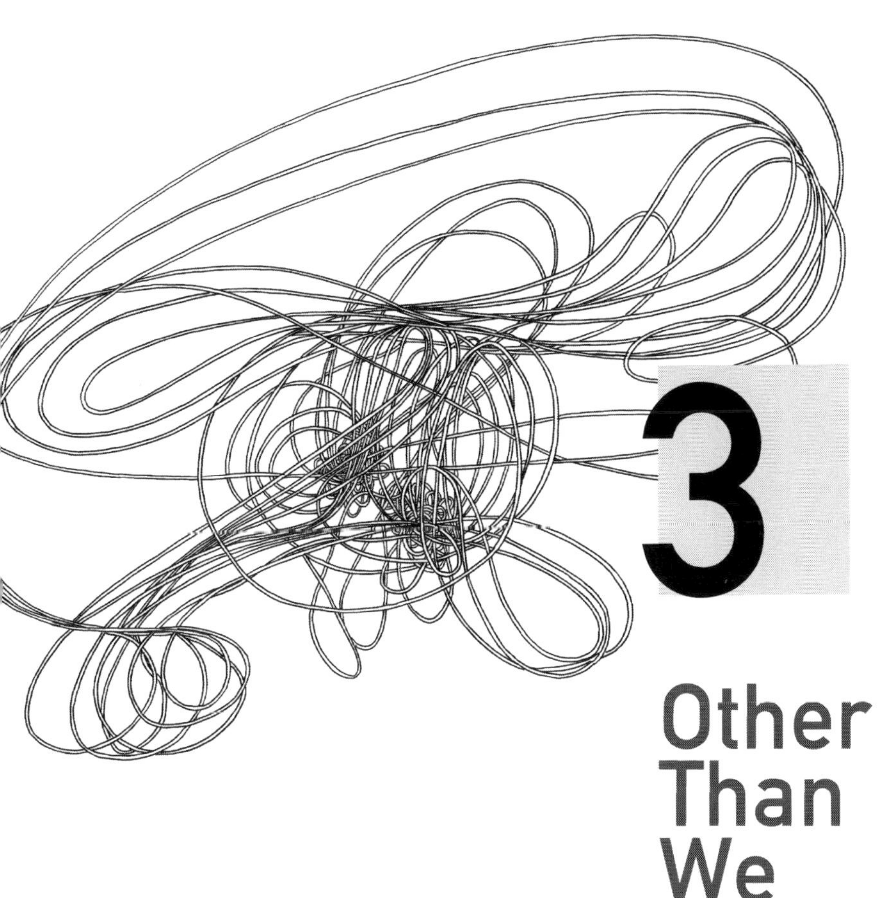

3

Other Than We

For Abel, Eben, Sirine,
Justice, Shami — our newbies —
and for their parents.

TIME

The Future, a few years after The Deluge, a full-scale climate disaster.

SETTING

Part I takes place inside The Dome, a hermetically sealed environment where the privileged remnants of society, plus a few refugees who work for them, now live.

Part II takes place in a clearing outside The Dome where a denuded nature is struggling to come back in late fall and winter, with 90-degree Fahrenheit heat. Also, in the back of a truck on a road during a storm, and in a cave.

Part III takes place in and around the clearing as spring with soaring temperatures approaches.

NOTES

On the text: The play proceeds on several levels. It is, at once, a cli-fi plot to create a new race, superior to Homo sapiens, capable of surviving in a harsh post-Deluge world; it is a discourse and debate on the origins of language and consciousness; and it is a recognizable drama of procreation, one in which the acts of birthing and nurturing, instead of fighting and killing, become heroic.

On the staging: Simplicity above all. No attempt at verisimilitude. A vista scene changes. Minimal props: a wine bottle, flask, pieces of paper, metal containers for sperm, a plastic bucket, chains, and four newbie babies with small hooves and tails: two for the nursing scene and two of which, newborns, emerge from Eve. Medical instruments are not necessary.

CHARACTERS

MICHELLE or MICK, an obstetrician-gynecologist

EVE, a neuroscientist demoted to the position of part-time lecturer

TANAKA, a refugee, formerly a physician, from far away, allowed into The Dome to do menial labor and so that the radiation concentration in his bones can be monitored and studied

OPA, a renowned public intellectual (inspired by Noam Chomsky), a linguist, and grandfather of Eve

THE NEWBIES, human-animal creations of Eve, Mick, and Tanaka, engineered to be able to survive in the harsh, new world – and to avoid the mistakes of Homo sapiens. They are seen as babies in the arms of their creators but in the final scene, they are heard and seen *only* as bright, colored lights circling Opa.

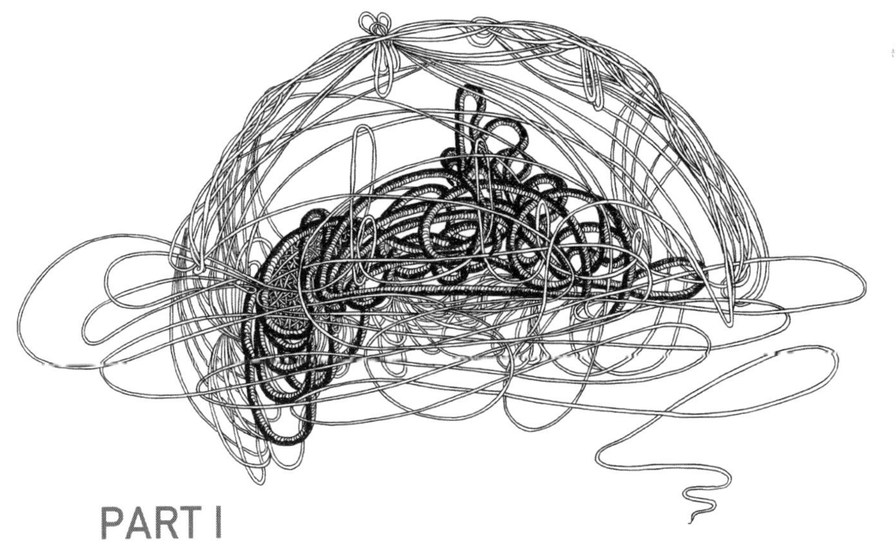

PART I

SCENE 1

[Inside The Dome in the bare room of Eve and Michelle. Michelle stands by the wall, looking out. Eve is still lying on a few blankets on the floor. From outside: the sounds of many shuffling feet, and a low dirge-like chant of many voices. A loudspeaker issues incoherent directives. There is a shot, a scream, momentary silence; the chant and marching pick up again.]

MICHELLE. Women are wearing out.

[Michelle takes a drink from an open wine bottle.]

EVE. Mick, it's 7 a.m.

MICHELLE. The dregs from last night.

[A mechanical beep, indicative of surveillance.]

EVE. *[Louder.]* Women are not wearing out.

MICHELLE. *[Louder.]* Of course not. You are obedient, still in bed.

EVE. I'm weeping.

MICHELLE. No, you are not.

EVE. Just wondering, what was weeping?

MICHELLE. When?

EVE. There was weeping.

MICHELLE. I'll open a new bottle.

[Eve gets up. She goes to Michelle.]

EVE. *[Nuzzling Michelle.]* Somewhere wild things are growing.

[A mechanical beep.]

MICHELLE. *[Louder, a truism.]* "Levels of radiation and pollutant particulates outside The Dome remain lethal."

EVE. Dream, must have been.

[*Eve hands Michelle a piece of paper. Michelle takes it and reads it intently during the following exchange.*]

MICHELLE. We're on the mandatory list to conceive, both of us.

EVE. It's what you do.

MICHELLE. Implant eggs into wombs.

EVE. That must be very satisfying for you.

MICHELLE. Precisely.

[*She is referring to the paper she is reading.*]

MICHELLE. Just here; is there a problem with that?

[*She shows the paper to Eve.*]

EVE. When looked at like this . . .

[*Eve lightly touches Michelle's head, heart, and womb area. Michelle understands Eve is speaking of creating head-heart connection.*]

MICHELLE. You mustn't think of it as a demotion.

EVE. Think again. I love lecturing.

MICHELLE. We are both quite on track.

[*Michelle quietly rips and then eats the piece of paper.*]

EVE. I think so.

MICHELLE. I do, absolutely.

[*She takes a large drink to wash the paper bits down.*]

EVE. So, darling, please don't drink so much.

MICHELLE. Off to work, us.

SCENE 2

[*Michelle, in their room, drinking from a bottle of red wine, as Eve enters with Tanaka standing some distance behind her.*]

MICHELLE. It's very good, this *Côtes du Rhône.*

EVE. Mick . . .

MICHELLE. I will ask for a case.

EVE. Amazing wine survived.

MICHELLE. Aged underground.

EVE. [*She goes closer, into Mick's ear.*] Is your phone off?

MICHELLE. Light, full-bodied, tart with a lemony tang.

EVE. "Lemony." What a nice word. Mick . . .

MICHELLE. Perhaps it's just chemicals.

EVE. Let me taste. [*She reaches inside Michelle's pocket, takes the phone out and turns it off.*] I scrubbed.

MICHELLE. All of a sudden her womb ruptured, 25 weeks. I did not say a thing. I pulled them out. Three fetuses, more or less, preemies, more and more. The brain is not fully developed. [*A mechanical beep.*] Still, we have made great advances. Artificial wombs would terminate the issue. But, the placenta, to date, is non-replicable.

EVE. Mick.

MICHELLE. And women without wombs, used wombs, used-up . . . exiled, poof, outside The Dome. I saved them. Not her. She bled out. Placenta goop. [*Beep.*] I am richly rewarded for my work with *Côtes du Rhône.* Wouldn't you like some wine?

EVE. Mick, my darling, hush.

MICHELLE. Do you know what we do to the motherless ones? Those born too soon. The deformed.

EVE. Hush, Mick.

MICHELLE. Direct from the womb to your dining room.

EVE. Ha, ha. Very clever.

MICHELLE. Solution to the increasing food shortage.

EVE. [*She waves him over.*] Mick.

[*Tanaka approaches. He bows slightly, his hands in prayer position at his heart.*]

MICHELLE. I am nauseous all the time now.

TANAKA. I believe we should walk.

[*They walk out.*]

[*They return in mid-conversation . . . They are on an empty street in The Dome.*]

TANAKA. Would be opened up . . .

MICHELLE. Theoretically.

EVE. Actually. If we did; when we do do.

TANAKA. On the cortex.

EVE. So that areas of the brain . . .

MICHELLE. Let him explain.

TANAKA. Quickly, naturally, with minimal risk, prenatally.

MICHELLE. We complete the evolutionary leap.

TANAKA. It's a simple extension of existing cortical wiring.

MICHELLE. Like flicking a switch.

EVE. Might have happened naturally all by itself.

MICHELLE. A roll of the evolutionary dice.

EVE. How ever did consciousness arise out of matter?

MICHELLE. From a glob of flesh, thought. Think of that.

EVE. Looking down, looking out, looking in for the first time.

TANAKA. All else, I believe, you've considered but this.

MICHELLE. And you can achieve . . .

TANAKA. Put together.

EVE. Unify, finally . . .

MICHELLE. . . . What might have been ripped, disrupted, hurt when the cortex . . .

EVE. Emerged . . .

TANAKA. Feeling and thought might be connected as was intended.

MICHELLE. Intended by who or what?

EVE. The Mind is the brain viewed from a distance.

TANAKA. From a distance, it is possible to see.

EVE. Totality.

MICHELLE. Where is he from? You, from where?

TANAKA. Far from here.

MICHELLE. Sent?

TANAKA. Fled.

MICHELLE. How did you get in?

TANAKA. They wish to measure the radiation content of my bones.

MICHELLE. Makes sense.

TANAKA. Of course, we won't know . . .

MICHELLE. Plausible, at best.

TANAKA. Nevertheless . . .

EVE. We shall try.

MICHELLE. We will.

TANAKA. If you wish.

MICHELLE. If not, I will be implanting dinner food into . . .

EVE. Stop it, Mick.

TANAKA. I have forgotten my past.

MICHELLE. As one must.

TANAKA. I am grateful, cheerful, obedient, industrious.

EVE. One of us.

TANAKA. Once a physician, I work as a janitor now.

[*He bows and they part. A moment later: Mick and Eve in their room.*]

EVE. He came to my lecture. Did I let a dangerous word slip? Is that why he came up?

MICHELLE. I don't think so.

EVE. You asked where he was from; you must have thought . . .

MICHELLE. Tastes just like chicken.

EVE. Stop that, please. I can't stand it.

MICHELLE. No one remembers what chicken tastes like.

EVE. Radiation-free puree is delicious.

MICHELLE. Running out.

EVE. He sought me out.

MICHELLE. I was there.

EVE. You were there?

MICHELLE. Where you couldn't see.

EVE. Why?

MICHELLE. I wanted to see. Hear, I mean.

EVE. You were checking up?

MICHELLE. We are coming too close to deciding, now.

EVE. You needed to know.

MICHELLE. I suppose so.

EVE. Who are you, really, Michelle?

MICHELLE. Who are you, Eve?

EVE. The woman who loves you. Your love.

MICHELLE. A dangerous thought.

EVE. They could do it that way.

MICHELLE. Send me.

EVE. Send you.

MICHELLE. Of course, they could.

EVE. You were in the hospital, delivering . . .

MICHELLE. I was not spying on you.

EVE. My darling. How could I think such a thing?

MICHELLE. You are suggestible.

EVE. I?

MICHELLE. Immediately, you doubted me.

EVE. You set me up.

MICHELLE. So has he.

EVE. He has offered himself.

MICHELLE. I am not convinced.

EVE. How could he think it all up?

MICHELLE. He is using their script.

EVE. They are on to us?

MICHELLE. If they are, they would send someone like him.

SCENE 3

[A hallway in the hospital: Tanaka, the janitor, is sweeping. Michelle enters, in scrubs.]

TANAKA. Doctor!

MICHELLE. Are you speaking to me?

TANAKA. Excuse me, please. You dropped this.

MICHELLE. I?

TANAKA. Yes, onto the floor. I was sweeping. Just as you walked by.

MICHELLE. I see.

TANAKA. Perhaps it is nothing. I thought, though, you might wish to have it. Forgive me. I am most sorry to have disturbed you.

MICHELLE. It's garbage, I'm sure.

TANAKA. In that case, allow me to dispose of it for you.

MICHELLE. I will take care of it myself. Thank you.

[She takes the paper quickly from him, opens it and reads.]

MICHELLE. Garbage, indeed.

[She stuffs the paper into her pocket.]

SCENE 4

[*Michelle enters their room and grabs the bottle of wine.*]

EVE. Is your phone off?

MICHELLE. Of course.

EVE. I scrubbed.

MICHELLE. That does it, then.

EVE. Should.

MICHELLE. Here, darling, a toast, to us. [*She drinks.*]

EVE. They've asked to talk with me about my research.

MICHELLE. Yours?

EVE. Ridiculous, isn't it?

MICHELLE. I suppose they are running out of suspects.

EVE. Thank you very much.

MICHELLE. I didn't mean that in a demeaning way.

EVE. You think you are smarter than I.

MICHELLE. More mechanistic, that's all.

EVE. I used to write on scraps, fold them up, stick them in cracks.

MICHELLE. I know how circumspect . . .

EVE. Someone in class denounced me.

MICHELLE. Little shit.

EVE. "Motherese" I was talking about. He said he signed up for a class in linguistics, not retro-feminism.

MICHELLE. Mother-ease has a nice ring.

EVE. I explained: The capacity for language comes hardwired in the brain.

MICHELLE. Still, if mothers do not speak to their children.

EVE. Language is delayed.

MICHELLE. So, you are pro-Motherese?

EVE. I said as little as I could. In that same class, Tanaka appeared.

MICHELLE. Can we trust him?

EVE. I trust him.

MICHELLE. He sticks out, in the back of your lecture.

EVE. But he's right.

MICHELLE. He's right all right.

EVE. We need him.

MICHELLE. Not if he's setting us up.

EVE. He can do what we need done, Michelle.

MICHELLE. I can, too, now, actually.

EVE. I don't think so.

MICHELLE. Thank *you*, very much.

EVE. You cannot operate on yourself. You cannot do that. On me, yes, of course.

MICHELLE. Why did he suddenly appear?

EVE. He found us, me, that is, took a risk.

MICHELLE. What risk did he take?

EVE. He engaged me in conversation.

MICHELLE. Why?

EVE. He's been coming to my class. At first, I thought just to sweep, straighten up. Then, suddenly it dawned.

MICHELLE. And, now, you've been denounced as some sort of feminist.

EVE. I say things I shouldn't, I know. I get carried away. But most of my students don't listen to what I say.

MICHELLE. Don't be so sure. If one denounces you.

EVE. A complaint, that's all.

MICHELLE. And here he comes offering . . .

EVE. Suggesting . . .

MICHELLE. It's too neat.

EVE. It looks like a trap.

MICHELLE. The missing link.

EVE. He thinks, that's all.

MICHELLE. He knows what we need to know.

EVE. Maybe so.

MICHELLE. I believe him, Eve.

EVE. I want to, Michelle.

MICHELLE. Believe me, then, do.

EVE. It's different than knowledge, belief.

MICHELLE. How did it end, the denouncing I mean.

EVE. But without belief, one cannot think. Without someone's adoring gaze, deep looks, in the crucial first 18 months of life outside the womb, the infant brain, we can say, literally freezes itself. The neurons fail to develop. The infant ceases to become. Babies raised as ours are . . .

MICHELLE. What was Motherese once, has become biological now.

EVE. *De-evolution* outside, also, inside the womb.

MICHELLE. It's possible – why shouldn't it be? – to lose what has developed over thousands and thousands of years, biologically speaking – empathy, imagination.

EVE. What's left is aggression.

MICHELLE. Increasing outbreaks of hate.

EVE. Depression.

MICHELLE. Better for being eaten, I suppose.

EVE. For eating, too, better not to know.

SCENE 5

[A hallway in the hospital. Tanaka, with dustpan and broom, pulls a trash bag. Michelle comes along, drinking wine from a flask. She bumps into him. Wine spills on her white coat.]

MICHELLE. Why can't you watch out!

[She looks around, terrified someone might be watching.]

TANAKA. I am sorry, Doctor. Forgive.

MICHELLE. You got your filth all over me.

TANAKA. Allow me to try.

[From his pocket, he takes a rag as if to rub out the stain.]

MICHELLE. Take your hands off me, scum!

TANAKA. I'm terribly sorry. It is a slight stain. Please. [*He hands her the rag.*] Take this, you can.

MICHELLE. More carelessness on your part, I will see you go back where you came from . . .

TANAKA. Thank you, Doctor. I understand.

[She leaves, clutching the rag in her hand.]

SCENE 6

[In their room. Michelle unwraps the rag Tanaka gave her. He had wrapped it about a metal vial of sperm, an old cocktail shaker, which she shows to Eve.]

MICHELLE. My phone is off. Yours?

EVE. I also scrubbed.

MICHELLE. High quality.

EVE. Are they his?

MICHELLE. You have a crush.

EVE. On you, yes.

MICHELLE. They are healthy. I can tell you that.

EVE. Maybe not his.

MICHELLE. Mixed. Animal. Man.

EVE. Which?

MICHELLE. Camel, I think, elephant, horse.

EVE. *Black Stallion*! How?

MICHELLE. There's a stash. Interspecies insemination, us.

EVE. It's the best time for us.

MICHELLE. Curious how that works.

EVE. Females in groups.

MICHELLE. Phases of the moon.

EVE. Pulling at us even though we can't see.

MICHELLE. So they'd all be nursing together.

EVE. If one needed more milk.

MICHELLE. If one mother didn't live.

EVE. He's pure, somehow.

MICHELLE. You do have a crush.

EVE. So do you.

MICHELLE. Don't get carried away.

EVE. We don't ask him anything, where he's from . . .

MICHELLE. He doesn't want to say.

EVE. When he's ready, perhaps.

MICHELLE. Later on, after . . .

[*A beep.*]

EVE. [*Louder.*] We are happy here.

MICHELLE. Of course we are.

EVE. We are on the list.

MICHELLE. We reproduce, they're done with us.

EVE. That's how it works?

MICHELLE. Weak wombs. Substandard eggs.

EVE. Nevertheless . . .

MICHELLE. We are doing our duty, gladly.

EVE. We offer ourselves . . .

MICHELLE. This morning two vials in dry ice were on my desk. Four-star variety.

[*She takes them out of her pockets.*]

EVE. For one's own, it is only natural to want.

MICHELLE. There is five stars, after that. I suppose four stars is all right.

EVE. We accept.

MICHELLE. We might have been asked to report.

EVE. Did you ask for the privilege?

MICHELLE. Now that you mention it, I cannot remember whether or not . . .

EVE. You must have asked, otherwise . . .

MICHELLE. I must have.

EVE. They granted your wish.

[*Michelle empties the two vials of "official sperm" into the garbage.*]

MICHELLE. [*She laughs.*] I'm honored, in fact.

EVE. A mark of respect.

MICHELLE. I am useful, yes. I fertilize. Put them in. Pull them out.

EVE. I'll fertilize yours.

MICHELLE. I will, too, you.

[*They nuzzle each other and laugh and shush their own laughter.*]

MICHELLE. First, I'm going to steal your eggs.

EVE. There were birds.

MICHELLE. When?

EVE. When there were eggs. "*My lark*," "*my dove*," lovers said.

MICHELLE. Birds coated with oil. Birds drowned in the slew.

EVE. Birds on the wing. Can one love without birds?

MICHELLE. We do.

EVE. Poets wrote about birds. If we had poems, would we have birds?

MICHELLE. We have plenty of eggs, my lark, my dove. I'm going to grab a handful.

EVE. That sort of thing turns you on.

MICHELLE. It does. We are on the list. It's allowed.

EVE. Mandated, in fact. Will you teach me how to do you?

MICHELLE. Can't.

EVE. Could.

MICHELLE. Someone else harvested mine.

EVE. "Harvested."

MICHELLE. Took them out.

EVE. I love the sounds of what was.

MICHELLE. I'll bring you to orgasm just before. The eggs excite.

EVE. Did "someone else" bring you to orgasm, Mick?

MICHELLE. I, myself, did.

EVE. My lark, my dove.

MICHELLE. I'll put them into a dish; show you how to insert a needle inside, squirt some sperm.

EVE. We can watch them divide.

MICHELLE. Indeed. There are a few simple adjustments to make in the healthy zygote. Before implantation, I mean.

EVE. Implantation, that's the sexy part.

MICHELLE. Extraction, fertilization, manipulation, implantation. [*In a low voice*] Additional manipulation in four months' time.

EVE. You love your work.

MICHELLE. I hate my work. I implant fertilized eggs. None of them take. She is exiled outside The Dome. Or she carries three or four, born premature to be mashed in a blender.

EVE. Please.

MICHELLE. I spoil your romantic mood.

EVE. They used to eat birds. Wring their necks. Pluck them and pull them apart. Roast them on a spit.

SCENE 7

[*Some months later. The three meet on a deserted street. Michelle and Eve are barely but noticeably pregnant. Michelle drinks from her flask. Floodlights sweep the area periodically. Sirens are heard.*]

EVE. Please, don't.

MICHELLE. A sip. I sip.

EVE. They've asked me for my research. [*Pause.*] They, the mythical "they," have asked. The authority, the authorities want. After my rebuke of several months back. [*Silence.*] Not asked, not precisely. Not exactly requested. In which case, I could say "no" politely. Subpoenaed. They have subpoenaed my work.

[*Michelle drinks.*]

EVE. Please, Mick.

MICHELLE. In Mediterranean countries, they drink.

EVE. Drank.

MICHELLE. Drank all the way through. [*She takes another drink.*] There were birds, too.

EVE. I feel quite, quite the thing, you know, the object, object of their, what?

MICHELLE. I don't think it should hurt. In moderation, all things. Please.

[*She puts the flask into her pocket.*]

EVE. They want my hard drive.

MICHELLE. What is on your hard drive?

EVE. Nothing, of course. How do I know?

MICHELLE. Why do they want what you have?

EVE. They were leaving me quite alone. Lecturer, not professor. Introductory only. Until Tanaka . . . I have no idea. Truly. None. The little shithe-

MICHELLE. Shsssh.

EVE. Student stopped coming to class after the Motherese fiasco. I stopped using the word. Apologized. But, of course, now [*she gestures toward her belly*] I am, we are both. How do they say, in the motherly way?

MICHELLE. On the list, both of us.

EVE. Who knows how that goes?

MICHELLE. One can't be sure. I cannot be, in any case.

EVE. Was it you, Tanaka?

MICHELLE. You know it wasn't him.

EVE. Let him answer for himself.

TANAKA. I have put myself at your mercy, as well.

[*Silence. They look at one another.*]

EVE. Michelle. It might have been. She's been jockeying for position. Has she not?

MICHELLE. Are you out of your mind? I, jockeying for what?

EVE. I saw you speaking to him.

MICHELLE. To whom?

EVE. To the director. That is *to whom.*

MICHELLE. I must speak to the director. I'm the liaison. You didn't want to do it yourself. Didn't want to get your hands dirty, I suspect, by speaking to the Di-Rec-Tor on our behalf.

TANAKA. Our behalf?

MICHELLE. Mine and hers. That's what liaisons do.

EVE. They liaison. Make liaisons. Allegiances come up.

TANAKA. They must.

EVE. When one speaks to the director on one's behalf.

MICHELLE. On our behalf, I was speaking to him.

EVE. There we are.

MICHELLE. You don't think that.

TANAKA. It might have been a slip of the tongue.

EVE. We're not actually accusing you.

MICHELLE. Accusing, that's *not* what you are doing?

TANAKA. Trying to get to the bottom of things.

EVE. The bottom, yes. They've subpoenaed *my* research; *my* entire computer, plus backup disks. That means they are on to us.

MICHELLE. I liaison to throw them off the track.

TANAKA. Do you?

MICHELLE. Of course I do. You chose me. Mechanistic Michelle.

TANAKA. Trustworthy.

EVE. Do they know about him?

MICHELLE. How would I know?

EVE. Did his name ever come up?

MICHELLE. It's not my fault I operate.

EVE. His name came up.

MICHELLE. I do not relish what I do.

TANAKA. It does come with a certain privilege.

MICHELLE. To liaison with the director? You consider that a privilege? You chose me.

EVE. We had no choice, really.

TANAKA. That is so.

EVE. Of course.

MICHELLE. Stop saying that.

EVE. If you do, I will.

MICHELLE. Who do you say is saying what?

EVE. Nothing is "of course." Nothing is predetermined to that extent.

TANAKA. It is because you are pregnant.

EVE. If Michelle did not betray me, that is.

MICHELLE. I defended you.

EVE. From what?

MICHELLE. *"Does she see the Old Man?"* the director asked.

EVE. Of course he did.

MICHELLE. *"Of course not,"* I said.

EVE. Of course.

MICHELLE. Said you were unfit to teach.

EVE. You gave him my research in my defense.

MICHELLE. I said, *"She's incredibly smart."*

EVE. You told him what's not on my hard drive.

MICHELLE. I did not.

EVE. You told him my theories, my thoughts.

MICHELLE. I said, *"She is smart but wrong."*

EVE. You told him my theories of Mind.

MICHELLE. I told him, *"She's gone off the track."*

EVE. You set me up.

MICHELLE. I said, *"She's unhinged."*

EVE. You think so.

MICHELLE. I do not.

EVE. You gave him enough.

MICHELLE. You will lose your job.

EVE. Exiled outside The Dome.

MICHELLE. I had to throw him a bone.

EVE. Bones. Mine.

TANAKA. We will be gone.

MICHELLE. He caught me off guard.

TANAKA. We will be safe. Outside.

EVE. Ha! [*Pause.*] They want my research.

TANAKA. Just to be sure.

MICHELLE. There is nothing on your hard drive.

TANAKA. Let us take a deep breath and move on.

[*They all breathe in and out, slowly and deeply.*]

EVE. Fine.

MICHELLE. It is because we are pregnant.

EVE. I don't want to do this.

MICHELLE. Eve . . .

EVE. [*Increasingly hysterical.*] I don't want my body like this. To be in this way. Belching, farting, full of gas. I don't want to be used by, invaded, a mother, what a stupid, insane, ridiculous, cruel thought, me. I never had a, I hated my, how could I, now I'm trapped, not myself, I am not, don't exist.

MICHELLE. I can take it out.

TANAKA. Please. I think . . .

EVE. You can't.

MICHELLE. I could.

EVE. I don't trust either of you. You've set me up.

TANAKA. I believe your pregnancy has been already noted.

MICHELLE. I will do an abortion.

TANAKA. Don't.

EVE. You can't. They know. I'm on the list. I can't stop, I'm, I'm not, I don't have a self, eaten up.

TANAKA. It's a natural feeling.

EVE. How would you know?

TANAKA. I have known women.

EVE. Known them, sure . . .

TANAKA. You won't really be a mother, you realize.

EVE. Okay, okay. I'm fine. Better now. It was . . .

MICHELLE. Such a fear washed over you.

EVE. That's what it was, not over, up, up from inside, as if . . .

MICHELLE. I know.

EVE. You do?

MICHELLE. The accusations take a toll.

EVE. They do.

MICHELLE. Not being trusted.

EVE. Is what they want.

TANAKA. But nothing is on your hard drive.

EVE. How do you know what is on *my* hard drive?

TANAKA. They want to know what you know about me.

EVE. What do they know about you?

MICHELLE. Absolutely nothing at all.

TANAKA. I passed Eve a USB stick in the hall.

EVE. You did not.

TANAKA. I put it into your pocket.

MICHELLE. I took it out that night.

EVE. You put me at risk and now they want my fucking research.

MICHELLE. I needed to see it written out.

EVE. My research I memorize.

MICHELLE. I destroyed the USB stick.

EVE. How do you do that?

MICHELLE. With a brick. I scattered the pieces as I walked.

EVE. We cannot go on like this.

TANAKA. You understood the procedure.

MICHELLE. It is so simple, elegant, it must be right, but now they have subpoenaed her research.

EVE. We don't need to keep saying that.

MICHELLE. You don't write anything down.

EVE. But you need to see things written out.

TANAKA. I had to share my thought.

EVE. Not on a USB stick, I do not.

MICHELLE. It's too early to do the procedure.

TANAKA. Can we wait a week?

MICHELLE. Even so . . .

EVE. I haven't given my hard drive to them . . . They've got it, of course.

MICHELLE. There is nothing on it.

EVE. You keep saying that. Somehow, I resent it.

MICHELLE. I meant written down.

EVE. My research happens to be of utmost importance.

TANAKA. To us, it is, yes.

MICHELLE. To them, too, I suppose.

EVE. They have found out where all the neural pathways reside.

MICHELLE. Great advance.

TANAKA. They will attach electrodes.

EVE. Read every brainwave, yes.

MICHELLE. Complete surveillance. Total.

EVE. They think the flesh is all there is.

MICHELLE. They want to know what you know.

EVE. Mind can resist. I know that much.

MICHELLE. They need to eradicate that.

TANAKA. Mind exists on the nonmaterial plain.

MICHELLE. Inaccessible to them.

TANAKA. The cortical extension we propose . . .

EVE. Must remain, so to speak, out of mind, if they are to exert full control.

MICHELLE. They will charge you with criminal intent.

EVE. Mind is what hasn't happened yet.

MICHELLE. Fomenting rebellion.

EVE. Mind is vision.

TANAKA. No matter how many brainwaves they colonize.

EVE. Neurons get fired up by being looked at.

TANAKA. I think it might be all right.

EVE. By being seen, does Mind come into being.

MICHELLE. They can't figure that out. Not by what I told them, they can't.

EVE. In the spaces between, Mind is.

TANAKA. I can do the procedure.

MICHELLE. I doubt that.

TANAKA. As we've agreed.

MICHELLE. It's too early; it won't stick.

TANAKA. If they're on to us, it will be too late.

MICHELLE. I'm sorry. I'm so sorry.

EVE. There's nothing to be sorry about.

MICHELLE. I'm sorry nevertheless. One can be innocent and sorry.

EVE. You are overemotional because you are pregnant.

MICHELLE. All right, I'm over it.

EVE. Good.

TANAKA. It is because of our sudden advance.

EVE. Mind force, ours.

[*Pause.*]

TANAKA. We're so close.

MICHELLE. Four months is the absolute minimum.

EVE. I have to get Opa.

TANAKA. It will be fine. I assure you.

EVE. Now, then, it has to be.

MICHELLE. I forbid.

EVE. You forbid?

MICHELLE. Eve.

EVE. Michelle.

TANAKA. I see it!

[*Silence.*]

TANAKA. I can do it, now.

EVE. Opa will say he knew all along. Opa can't stand not to be the smartest person around.

TANAKA. I am most eager to meet him.

[*They leave in different directions.*]

SCENE 8

[A few days later. Dark, door opens; an empty examination room.]

TANAKA. I need a light.

[He flicks a switch. Bright lights come on.]

TANAKA. Clean. I know where things are.

MICHELLE. Eve should be here.

TANAKA. There's the table. Lie down, Michelle, please.

[Michelle lies down on the table. Tanaka performs the procedure with his back to the audience, working intently, bent over her.]

MICHELLE. Laparoscopic.

TANAKA. Will not hurt too much. I hope not.

MICHELLE. I can endure it.

TANAKA. We will talk as I work. Check the list.

MICHELLE. Radiation resistance.

TANAKA. Heat tolerance to 135 degrees Fahrenheit.

MICHELLE. Ouch.

TANAKA. Sorry.

MICHELLE. I meant that hot?

TANAKA. It's September, now, 90-plus degrees outside The Dome.

MICHELLE. Fast on their feet.

TANAKA. Two or four legs as they choose.

MICHELLE. Hands with opposable thumbs. Arms.

TANAKA. Large water storage capacity.

MICHELLE. Herbivores.

TANAKA. Omnivores when and if.

MICHELLE. Androgynous.

TANAKA. We intend.

MICHELLE. Can you see where the cortex might be?

TANAKA. I can.

MICHELLE. Where is Eve?

TANAKA. Don't move. There.

MICHELLE. Thought connected to the gut-brain.

TANAKA. I reinforce the vestigial empathy centers, just here.

MICHELLE. Good.

TANAKA. I believe so.

MICHELLE. We've done it, then. [*She sits up.*] Head-heart connection.

TANAKA. Perhaps so. [*He takes her hands in his.*]

[*Eve enters, distressed. Her shirt is bloody.*]

EVE. I'm late.

MICHELLE. [*She sits up on the table.*] Where are you hurt?

TANAKA. [*He knows immediately.*] It's not her blood.

EVE. Outbreak of hate.

MICHELLE. All the time now.

[*Eve climbs onto the table.*]

EVE. Dark-skinned man on the street. Angry guy pulls out a knife: *"Dome belongs to people like me."* Throat slashed. Falls into me. On the ground, on top. If it had been you, Mick, you would have stuck your finger in the right spot. Like a geyser. Blood spurting. Him choking. *"Tell everyone that I love them,"* he says. Dies in my lap.

MICHELLE. Please, take that shirt off.

EVE. Left him on the street. Ran.

MICHELLE. His body, you mean.

TANAKA. You were there for him.

MICHELLE. All right, my love.

[*Michelle motions to take off the bloody shirt.*]

EVE. It's his blood. Let it stay.

MICHELLE. Darling, you were wonderful, brave.

EVE. Neck slashed on the street.

MICHELLE. The hate comes boiling, flooding up.

EVE. A geyser it was.

TANAKA. We must do the procedure.

MICHELLE. Darling, yes, lie down.

EVE. Oh, no, do you think I might lose them? Women do, shock. In shock. Shocked. I don't want to lose them. I need to tell them what he said. "*Tell your child, I love.*"

TANAKA. You will not lose them.

EVE. I feel cramping.

MICHELLE. We need to fix a few things.

EVE. What, what things?

MICHELLE. We've talked this through.

TANAKA. So the ones inside you might be.

EVE. Proof. We are not liable to control. He was not. Geysers of hate are not enough. *"Tell everyone I love them."* Can you make that happen with a needle inside an egg?

TANAKA. We can optimize chances.

EVE. They will need us, even so.

SCENE 9

[Opa sits in an old, ragged easy chair with a pile of journals, newspapers, magazines, and books, in his room. He is immersed in reading. Eve enters from behind, climbing through the window, so he cannot see her.]

EVE. [*Softly.*] Opa, tell me a story.

OPA. [*As if dreaming.*] A story.

EVE. About the bad days when you were a boy but everyone was good. There was no food. There was no work. But everyone was nice.

OPA. There was hope.

EVE. Hope.

[He stares straight out. Eve puts her hands over his eyes from behind the chair.]

EVE. Shssh. [*She whispers.*] I'm back.

OPA. How did you get in?

EVE. The night guard, one of them.

OPA. [*He whispers.*] Is one of us . . .

[She goes around the chair and takes his face in her hands.]

EVE. Hello, Opa.

[She kisses him on the forehead.]

OPA. Evie. We thought you'd gone over to . . .

EVE. Why not? Mother did.

OPA. Your mother bought our way into The Dome with her doomed marriage, if that's what you mean.

EVE. I'm not grateful, if that's what you expect.

OPA. How could you leave us like that? She . . .

EVE. I know.

OPA. Even after you said those things, she wanted to see you.

EVE. I couldn't, Opa. I was busy with work . . .

OPA. Work . . . You hurt her so, Evie.

EVE. Your house is always watched.

OPA. Of course.

EVE. They needed to think . . . I needed to convince them that . . .

OPA. She loved you. She wanted to see you once before . . .

EVE. Sure. I know. [*Silence.*]

OPA. It was painful and quick.

EVE. I am sorry, Opa.

OPA. I'm certain you are.

EVE. [*She laughs.*] Do you still walk, Opa?

OPA. I can walk, of course.

EVE. It's all right. We can sit.

[*She puts her hands under his arms to help him, and he gets up out of the chair.*]

OPA. What about? [*He looks around at everything.*]

[*They begin walking, slowly, with Eve holding his arm, and he sees she is pregnant.*]

OPA. Evie, look at you. You are.

EVE. I am.

OPA. But who? I thought . . .

EVE. Right.

OPA. Whoever is fine.

EVE. It's not done that way anymore.

OPA. With bodies, sweat.

EVE. Needles, Petri dishes.

OPA. Why has it always been you? Whatever you asked me to do.

EVE. Forever, Opa, we always said.

OPA. You were gone so long.

EVE. Back now. I won't leave you again.

OPA. They let me work here, undisturbed. I can broadcast, outside The Dome.

EVE. I know that. That's good. [*She moves him toward the door.*] Some people somewhere listen to you, if there are people somewhere else.

OPA. The act of speaking remains oddly satisfying. Clears my head.

EVE. The tapes might exist.

OPA. I, anyway, have a full set. Here is my latest: "*Life inside The Dome is increasingly untenable. We need not speak about the food, the rumors everyone has heard of what it contains. More lethal, though not remarked upon: The aquifer upon which The Dome was built has all but run out. This has not been made public knowledge as of yet. Purification of the same air, likewise, is no longer sustainable. Life inside The Dome for the privileged few is likely to cease far before . . .*"

EVE. Here, Opa, I'm here. [*She guides him toward the door.*] I'm not leaving you.

[*She indicates the way out with her head.*]

OPA. You're a neural scientist. I assume you are in the authorities' employ.

[*He stops.*]

EVE. A lecturer, merely.

OPA. You are more brilliant than that.

EVE. I always hated it when you and mother . . . brilliant. So what?

[*She moves him, again toward the door.*]

OPA. Better than not.

[*He stops.*]

EVE. Sure enough. Brilliant, *for* what.

[*Again, she indicates, come on.*]

OPA. You have always had your way with me.

[*He gives in. He is going with her.*]

EVE. I always thought you were a wise old owl watching over me.

OPA. Hooting: *"Who, who, what, what. Where are you?"*

EVE. Let's not speak anymore, dearest Opa. Let's just be quiet and sit. Let me rest my head on your lap.

[*Eve leads Opa out the door.*]

PART II

SCENE 10

[Michelle and Tanaka have made it outside The Dome to the clearing he passed on his way in, and which he seeded. Michelle is quite a bit more pregnant; she wears a loose dress. Her hair is loose. She is barefoot with a plastic bucket. Outside is a bleak landscape but with some vegetation.]

MICHELLE. Ramps, fiddleheads, asparagus, purslane. There might be mushrooms in many varieties — chanterelle, porcine, bolete, morels. Eve loved the sounds of food, "lemony." Strawberries low to the ground. We can live. There is natural radiation in fungi. It will build their resistance.

TANAKA. Eve is not here.

MICHELLE. I know Eve is not here. Strange, isn't it? I ought to miss her.

TANAKA. You do not?

MICHELLE. I'm happy. Who wouldn't be? Aren't you? I never actually thought I'd see earth, sky. Live in the woods. Strange how familiar it feels. I saw a cardinal this morning. At least a red bird, maybe. A flash of red in the sky.

TANAKA. This spot was spared the worst.

MICHELLE. We'll have mugwort and peppermint for tea; they act medicinally. Nettles, watercress, scape, arugula, dandelion leaves. A salad, just think. (She puts her hand on her belly.) How could I not be happy, Tanaka?

TANAKA. Without Eve?

MICHELLE. Where were you, Tanaka, when it happened? On the other side?

TANAKA. I think there weren't sides.

MICHELLE. I'm sorry, of course not.

TANAKA. I came this way, on my way. A family had taken refuge here. It's a gentle spot. They had built themselves the shelter we use. I buried their bones. Over that rise is the wreck of their . . . one of those huge cars. What did they call them?

MICHELLE. SUVs.

TANAKA. When it happens to you there isn't time. You hope that later someone might come along.

MICHELLE. Oh, Tanaka.

TANAKA. To do something with the bones.

MICHELLE. Say a prayer, I wonder to whom.

TANAKA. I seeded this spot.

MICHELLE. Where our children will be born.

TANAKA. I don't think of them as "ours."

MICHELLE. Not children, either, I suppose.

TANAKA. I carried seeds in my pockets. I hoped, sometime . . .

MICHELLE. You could seed the land. For your family, Tanaka?

TANAKA. We require Eve, and the wise man.

MICHELLE. The Underground wanted him to teach the refugees stuck in the nether-space outside The Dome. You told me yourself. I'd make a ramp tart; I would need milk, butter, eggs. We'd need chickens, a cow.

TANAKA. Boil ramps, asparagus, fiddle heads. Be happy for a while, at least, content. Feel sun on your face.

MICHELLE. I was standing in the sun. There, at my feet, asparagus stalks. I bent; the earth smelled like sex.

[*Tanaka turns away from her.*]

MICHELLE. If we had salt.

TANAKA. Salt?

MICHELLE. Salt, Tanaka, did you ever taste?

TANAKA. I had a grandmother, too.

MICHELLE. *"Pinch of salt, add."*

TANAKA. The same in each language.

MICHELLE. Tanaka, take these two stalks. Put them into my vagina.

[*He remains with his back turned.*]

TANAKA. They will taste good as they are.

MICHELLE. Salt, Tanaka, salt. Think of salt.

[*He turns.*]

MICHELLE. You remember the taste.

[*He says nothing.*]

MICHELLE. Take two. Swirl them in me. Salt. Salt of the sea.

[*She turns her back to him. He lifts her skirt, puts two into her vagina. Hands her one. They each take a bite and then begin to eat, in silence.*]

MICHELLE. Think of it, Tanaka: Suddenly, without warning, a lump of flesh saw itself.

TANAKA. Matter convulsed and writhed with self-knowledge.

MICHELLE. Felt not just hunger or pain. Felt feelings, we might say.

TANAKA. Felt Self. Spoke.

MICHELLE. Flesh became conscious being looking out.

TANAKA. At first there was only all-knowing. A universe humming.

MICHELLE. That sounds strikingly like God.

TANAKA. God is what unified consciousness came to be called, or the gods – forces residing in us we once resided in.

MICHELLE. Life first knew of itself as unified being.

TANAKA. Did not *know,* rather was. Knowing implies not being able to know. Separateness, most of all.

MICHELLE. But, they will know more than we.

TANAKA. How could they?

MICHELLE. They will know peace within themselves.

TANAKA. They might dwell more completely in uncertainty. If they are not afraid to fear, that is my hope.

MICHELLE. But they will be more tender than we, tenderer they will be. Tender, shall I name one of mine?

TANAKA. Tender. Yes.

MICHELLE. They will live long lives, running free, Tender, and, I don't yet know.

TANAKA. You need not name.

MICHELLE. Perhaps, it's bad luck?

TANAKA. Wait till you see them.

MICHELLE. It doesn't matter, does it, what happens to us once it's done.

TANAKA. I think not.

MICHELLE. They won't need us much.

TANAKA. They might not relate to us at all.

MICHELLE. Oh. Oh, well. As long they're healthy, you know.

TANAKA. Smart and strong.

MICHELLE. As long as they're good.

TANAKA. It is what parents always have wished.

MICHELLE. Then why did it happen as it did?

TANAKA. Evolution got stuck.

MICHELLE. We are not parents, really.

TANAKA. Carriers, merely, nurturers, maybe.

MICHELLE. They won't be like . . . They will be . . .

TANAKA. Other than we.

SCENE 11

[Eve and Opa are in the back of an old truck, a tarp over their heads. It is raining hard and the truck is rumbling along a dark two-lane road at night.]

EVE. We have no idea, none, what actually is the nature of the creatures who are inside us. Who will they be, why and what for? I find this miraculous.

OPA. Foolhardy. Outright dangerous.

EVE. All pregnant women, I think, feel this way. Felt, I should say.

OPA. I am aghast, Evie.

EVE. Don't be, Opa.

OPA. To do this in your own body, to your own self.

EVE. We had no choice.

OPA. To do it to others is unforgiveable.

EVE. I wish the rain would stop.

OPA. I worry for you on these rough roads.

EVE. I worry about you catching a chill.

OPA. Snuggle up.

[They do.]

EVE. Like when I was little. You'd tell me something wonderful. We'd snuggle up.

[Silence.]

EVE. I'm so hungry. In the country . . .

OPA. If there is country.

EVE. A spot somewhere, more or less radiation free. Less immediately lethal, anyway, where we can stay for a bit. A spot nestled in hills; Tanaka saw it on his way. We might be able to eat food.

OPA. You think there will be food?

EVE. Mick knows how to gather things in from the woods.

OPA. I would like to eat a wild strawberry once again, feel that explosion on my tongue. You have no idea, do you, Evie, what that's like.

EVE. I suppose sex is . . .

OPA. Yes, of course, somewhat.

[*Pause.*]

EVE. What is better, Opa? Wild strawberries or sex?

OPA. It was a film. You wouldn't know.

EVE. Tell!

[*Silence.*]

OPA. I'm too worried about you.

EVE. Truly, I thought you'd be pleased.

OPA. How could you think such a thing?

EVE. Because something had to be done.

OPA. That does not make it advisable, nor doable.

EVE. What do you suggest? Resistance? Populist uprising?

OPA. You know who I am. What I say.

EVE. It didn't happen.

OPA. Might someday.

EVE. The human brain can devolve. Has.

[*Silence.*]

OPA. Human action, perhaps, not the *ability* to think.

EVE. Where does thought come from, Opa?

OPA. Did thought create language or vice versa? We have no idea.

EVE. This leap of self outside the self that allows the self all of a sudden to look in . . .

OPA. Michelangelo's hand of God.

EVE. What?

OPA. The ceiling painting on the Sistine Chapel. An old man reached down from the heavens. Quite literal the fresco was. He extended his finger toward young Adam . . .

EVE. And then?

OPA. Then was the Renaissance, Evie. Looking out, looking in. An explosion of thought. Patriarchal, of course. Useful, nevertheless.

EVE. The brain rewired itself.

OPA. Perhaps. The man on the ceiling is inventing the god who animated him.

EVE. Mick and Tanaka could tell precisely which neural pathways required extension, making my theory flesh. Is that not amazing!

OPA. Wiggle, jiggle, I am going to jump from this truck.

EVE. Opa, sit.

OPA. I'm not a dog, nor is thought a switch you can turn on and off. Nor a piece of the puzzle called brain your friends can *manipulate*.

EVE. We know what we're doing, Opa.

OPA. Impossible!

EVE. You believe in stumbling along, exhorting others to change.

OPA. I am a very old man.

EVE. And I'm young. I can't wait.

OPA. To ruin your life, as your mother feared you would do.

EVE. Mother was jealous of me.

OPA. She knew you better than I.

EVE. Oh, yes, you always defended me.

OPA. Now, I am finally horrified, yes.

EVE. You admit you know nothing, yet you judge.

OPA. You kidnapped me.

EVE. We need you.

OPA. Nonsense.

EVE. There is a Mind we can access, Opa, over us. A think-feel Mind of the universe. I believe I could have proved it someday. I believe we have put it in them. Rewired their brains so they will know they belong. It is marvelous, truly.

OPA. Evie, you've stuffed your own belly. You will give birth to who knows what. Mute, ignorant beasts, who may suffer terribly.

EVE. Or eat us up.

OPA. A bad fairy tale.

EVE. They will speak.

OPA. Babble, perhaps, snort.

EVE. Our best knowledge, empirical and not, suggests we are advancing life.

OPA. By creating predators for Homo sapiens.

EVE. If any of our sort remain, we won't be able to take over again.

OPA. Species-cide. How can you be party to that?

EVE. They'll have four legs, Opa, plus arms, hands. They'll be able to run like the wind. Nature's coming back. To my speech, I mean. What a lovely expression that.

OPA. Stop! I can't anymore.

EVE. Opa! Your heart!

OPA. Yes.

EVE. Oh, no, Opa, let me massage.

OPA. I am the last . . .

EVE. Opa, breathe . . .

OPA. Who knows Aristotle, Von Humboldt, Spinoza, the rest . . . Who can think alongside the past. [*He composes himself.*] The loss, it overwhelmed me, that's all.

EVE. But that's why we need you. To give them what was. But, Opa, you absolutely must include women.

OPA. Of course, Simone Weil, [*pause*] Angela Davis. [*Then, he's at a loss.*] Toni Morrison!

EVE. We need you to tell our story to them.

OPA. You assume they will comprehend.

EVE. They can.

OPA. So they won't eat us up.

EVE. Don't give them ideas, Opa. Babies can hear in the womb.

OPA. Babies. My God.

EVE. They will be.

OPA. Cuddly babies with hooves.

EVE. That is how I see them myself. With bright eyes.

OPA. Horns.

[*The truck stops.*]

EVE. They will take us no further than this. Come, Opa, we need to get out.

OPA. We'll die on the road.

EVE. There's a cave. We can find it with our hands.

OPA. And Tanaka will come, sometime.

EVE. I'm starved. There will be provisions inside.

OPA. Are you sane, Eve? Are you any longer in your right mind?

EVE. I'm not my mother, Opa. Don't fear. Tanaka was here before us. That means he knows where we are.

SCENE 12

[*Michelle and Tanaka outside in the clearing.*]

MICHELLE. Have you ever lain with someone in the grass?

TANAKA. I have lain with a woman in the grass.

MICHELLE. I'm too big to lie down, I'm afraid.

TANAKA. I can come to you from behind.

MICHELLE. Like the asparagus, yes . . . Perhaps, we can jump-start the labor this way.

TANAKA. If your labor starts, they'll be born by the time Eve and the Old Man arrive.

MICHELLE. And if the labor doesn't begin?

TANAKA. Eve will come.

MICHELLE. I don't want Eve to know.

TANAKA. You want me once, that's all?

MICHELLE. I don't know. I haven't had you once yet.

TANAKA. And if I want you more?

MICHELLE. I'd feel desired, for a change.

TANAKA. Eve doesn't make you feel that way?

MICHELLE. I desired Eve. Now, it seems, I desire you.

TANAKA. I've not been desired for a long time.

MICHELLE. Perhaps you didn't know.

TANAKA. I've not desired desire.

MICHELLE. You've regenerated, too, here in the wild.

TANAKA. My feet in the mud. My sex rose.

MICHELLE. I, too, even so pregnant, I feel my flesh thudding.

TANAKA. They are on the road. I'm getting signals transmitted.

MICHELLE. They'll come soon.

TANAKA. Well, then?

MICHELLE. Yes, let's.

[*Pause.*]

TANAKA. It's not so easy to do.

[*Pause.*]

MICHELLE. How will I feed two?

TANAKA. We will all feed them. We will turn ourselves into milk. I know the way.

MICHELLE. That's how it will end.

TANAKA. For you and me.

MICHELLE. Not them.

TANAKA. The Old Man and Eve, if . . .

MICHELLE. Opa, too?

TANAKA. I need everyone's flesh. Besides, I believe he will want to know what it feels like.

MICHELLE. Turning ourselves into milk.

TANAKA. There is no other way with such limited food.

MICHELLE. Come into me, now, Tanaka, please. I want to know it all. The wind in my hair, grass stuck to my legs. The smells. A man's member inside. Yours.

SCENE 13

[*A few days later. The cave. There is a flickering fire. Eve and Opa pass a can with a spoon back and forth, eating what's left.*]

EVE. It's the same goop.

OPA. What did you expect?

EVE. Something from there.

OPA. Where?

EVE. Where they are. Something green, garlicky tasting.

OPA. You remember such things?

EVE. Mick told me I tasted garlicky.

OPA. I see.

EVE. Don't be squeamish, Opa.

OPA. Pass the purée.

EVE. I wonder if it really is "radiation free."

OPA. It's comforting.

EVE. I wonder if this can contains baby flesh.

OPA. Please.

EVE. The world is ripe for rewilding, Opa.

OPA. And you have the plan.

EVE. Not for us. For them.

OPA. You don't want to live?

EVE. Every pregnant woman in the history of the world has wanted to live, but not for herself so much. In the future, women will not bear the whole burden. Each one will be able to carry children.

OPA. It cannot come to good.

EVE. But it can.

OPA. It's no better than the geo-engineering that sped the final collapse.

EVE. We knew that wouldn't work.

OPA. These *things* inside of you will be superior to us?

EVE. They will know how to think about life.

OPA. *Think*, Evie, please.

EVE. They will not feel separate, apart.

OPA. They are animals, at best.

EVE. As are we, at best.

OPA. Biological organisms.

EVE. Of course, but if we have succeeded, they will know more than we.

OPA. What exactly will they *know*?

EVE. We reorganize flesh in order to reach beyond, truly, Opa, in order to grasp the role of the thinking-self in a feeling universe.

OPA. That's very nice.

EVE. It is, yes.

OPA. Except we are not talking philosophy here. You intend to birth these *things*.

EVE. What else could I do, now, with them?

OPA. Abort.

EVE. Forget that, and not *things*, please. Newbies is how I think of them. They do bear your remarkable genes.

OPA. And yours?

EVE. Mick's and Tanaka's as well, prime DNA. Animal genes, too.

OPA. This is madness, Evie.

EVE. They will need you to teach them how to think, what to think of.

OPA. You are desperate. You've unhinged yourself.

EVE. I've unhinged myself from what was.

OPA. We have no more food.

EVE. Tanaka will come.

OPA. And you want to live.

EVE. You think I'm not scared?

OPA. I hope you are.

EVE. Terrified.

OPA. Oh, my dear.

EVE. I'd like to rip out my belly.

OPA. Evie.

EVE. Yes. End this. I am going to die.

OPA. So are we all.

EVE. I know, but I don't know, do I? Do any of us actually think so?

OPA. Not even me at my age.

EVE. So. There we are.

OPA. But you have inflicted upon yourself . . .

EVE. What?

OPA. Something you believe in very much.

EVE. Believe with me, Opa, please.

OPA. I will try, because I believe in you, always have.

EVE. The rain has stopped. We could meet Tanaka on the road.

OPA. I don't walk very well. You go.

EVE. Nonsense, Opa. I'm not leaving you.

SCENE 14

[In their hut: Tanaka fiddles with an instrument. Michelle, enormously pregnant.]

TANAKA. They've stopped moving.

MICHELLE. They move all the time.

TANAKA. No movement at all.

MICHELLE. They've been kicking up a storm. There! Did you see that?

TANAKA. I did.

[Back to the instrument.]

MICHELLE. They're fine.

TANAKA. Why can't you think of someone besides yourself for a change?

MICHELLE. Myself! Why the fuck didn't you get yourself pregnant? Mr. Androgynous-Male! You think I'm thinking of myself. Go to hell.

TANAKA. Calm yourself down. It's not good for them.

MICHELLE. I am calm. Calm and huge and full of kicks. What do you know of any of that? I am out of shape. Look at me, for God's sake. You can't even bear the sight of me anymore. I'm a freak.

TANAKA. I am not talking about you.

MICHELLE. I can barely bend to gather in food. I squat.

TANAKA. I am speaking of Eve and the Old Man.

MICHELLE. Then, I cannot get up.

TANAKA. They've stopped moving. That's what I said.

MICHELLE. What does that mean?

TANAKA. I've lost the signal. It's gone dead.

MICHELLE. So you don't know if they are moving or not.

TANAKA. I think I can find them. I will find them and get them out.

MICHELLE. Out?

TANAKA. If they have been detained.

MICHELLE. Don't tell me that. I'm due any moment.

TANAKA. I know.

MICHELLE. Well, I don't know, actually. I'll just have to wait, that's all.

TANAKA. I do not believe that it's a matter of rational thinking, just deciding to wait.

MICHELLE. I can wait. How far away are they?

TANAKA. A couple of days perhaps.

MICHELLE. I should come with you.

TANAKA. That's not wise. I've alerted our friends in the resistance.

MICHELLE. And?

TANAKA. No answer from anyone.

MICHELLE. Perhaps they weren't friends.

TANAKA. I didn't want to upset you.

MICHELLE. It's the truth, isn't it?

TANAKA. I thought, perhaps we should let them go.

MICHELLE. Go where?

TANAKA. Fend for themselves.

MICHELLE. How can you say that?

TANAKA. Because of you, Michelle.

MICHELLE. What do I have to do with it?

TANAKA. Don't be coy.

MICHELLE. Not me, precisely, your precious creations inside my belly.

TANAKA. Yours, too.

MICHELLE. Eve's.

[*Silence.*]

TANAKA. I can stay with you. Deliver them.

MICHELLE. Something would remain.

TANAKA. That's right.

MICHELLE. And Eve?

TANAKA. We wait.

MICHELLE. Hope for the best.

TANAKA. Sacrifice is forbidden.

MICHELLE. Forbidden by whom?

TANAKA. By all that we live for.

MICHELLE. Sacrifice of what? Eve. The person I love. Her children.

TANAKA. They are not exactly hers. She is incubating them.

MICHELLE. Women have delivered alone. Throughout time. In fields, in the rain, on the run. In the midst of shelling, starvation.

TANAKA. Delivered human children.

MICHELLE. I'm healthy. I can.

TANAKA. Women have never delivered what you have inside.

MICHELLE. There is always a first time. I think for every woman it is always the first time.

TANAKA. I could take them out, now, then go.

MICHELLE. It's premature.

TANAKA. We don't know.

MICHELLE. I've absolutely no labor signs.

TANAKA. I'll stay and wait. Eve and the Old Man would understand.

MICHELLE. We had an idea, a plan. It depends upon us all.

TANAKA. I'm going to go. We're agreed.

MICHELLE. I will wait. Gather food in. I will be happy alone in the woods. I will nest.

TANAKA. You are eight and a half months.

MICHELLE. I could go nine, ten, even twelve. Bigger than a house. Who knows how long their actual gestation is.

TANAKA. I'll go, then.

MICHELLE. Bring them home. Here, I mean. Home, yes, for a minute, a few months, let's have a home on earth.

TANAKA. If they are still . . .

MICHELLE. If!

TANAKA. There is no signal, I said. I have to get them out before . . .

MICHELLE. Before?

TANAKA. A turncoat earns their way back into The Dome by doing them in.

MICHELLE. Why are you standing here? Go.

SCENE 15

[*The cave, a few days later.*]

OPA. Chained to a cave wall.

EVE. Without water or food.

OPA. We've been betrayed.

EVE. Not by Tanaka, not by him.

OPA. Who knows?

EVE. We will nevermore know anything soon.

OPA. Who knows what we'll know.

EVE. You believe thought remains. Somewhere outside us? That's funny, Opa, truly.

OPA. It was unprecedented in history. Human thought failed. We became incapable of knowing what we had to know.

EVE. That's it, Opa. Mind atrophied.

OPA. It seemed to me, suddenly, I suppose, that the human capacity for thought must have been tied all along to nature's capacity to stabilize itself. Perhaps, yes, there was a larger thinking mind at work. I've not yet come to clear conclusions on any of this; nevertheless, it seems to be a train of thought worth pursuing.

EVE. You've come over to our side, Opa, in the night.

OPA. Quite right. Now, ask your Universal Mind to undo these chains.

EVE. Of course, it can't.

OPA. Material reality triumphs once again, as objectively speaking material reality always does.

EVE. We are prisoners of those who thought prisons up.

OPA. You were quite small. Do you remember the songs . . .

EVE. We used to sing, you, mother, and me, when I got scared.

OPA. [*Sings.*] "*Viva La Quince Brigada*

EVE. [*Joins in.*] *Rúmbala, rúmbala, rúmbala.*

Viva La Quince Brigada

Rúmbala, rúmbala, rúmbala.

They came to stand beside the Spanish people

Rúmbala, rúmbala, rúmbala.

To try to stem the rising fascist tide

Rúmbala, rúmbala, rúmbala.

Let us all remember them tonight.

Rúmbala, rúmbala, rúmbala."

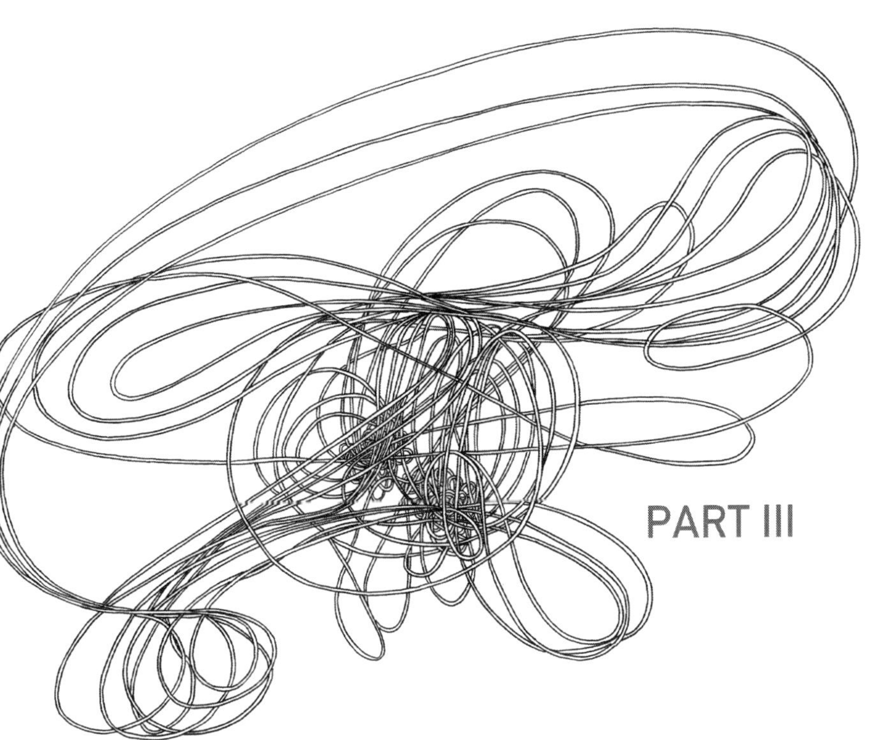

PART III

SCENE 16

[*Michelle is on a pallet bed. Eve, very pregnant, paces, her hands on her back.*]

EVE. We were in a cave without even water.

MICHELLE. Poor Eve.

EVE. What about you?

MICHELLE. Here I am, fine.

EVE. We were chained to the wall, legs and arms.

MICHELLE. The exiles are trained to do such things?

EVE. To get food, or to get back inside.

MICHELLE. They're very sweet, aren't they?

EVE. Very sweet. Tanaka and Opa are entranced.

MICHELLE. We're halfway there.

EVE. They are nursing them, now. We found you on the floor in a diabetic coma.

MICHELLE. Half are still inside. But alive.

EVE. Alive. All of us. First of all, I thought, never mind.

MICHELLE. Go ahead, tell me.

EVE. It's too much.

MICHELLE. It's good for you to talk. I'm interested, too. It happened to you.

EVE. Yes, well, it was freezing. Our limbs began to cramp. We both began to think, this is it, we are going die here. And, therefore, quite naturally, it seemed, Opa began to sing.

[*She sings and drums on her big belly.*]

"Viva La Quince Brigada

Rúmbala, rúmbala, rúmbala."

We were starving, freezing. We could not move. But we began to feel connected to a lineage. We stopped thinking about dying. It felt more as if we were about to be swept up into large, warm arms. There were voices all around harmonizing. Echoes bouncing off the cave walls. I began to look forward to it, really. I thought soon all this unpleasantness will be over. I'll be with my own kind. Opa was ecstatic. He began to see people he used to know. He sat up straight, a great smile on his face, singing alongside them. There were so many brave, smart people Opa saw on the other side. It would be like going home.

MICHELLE. You really think so?

EVE. I have no idea at all.

MICHELLE. You were hallucinating, in a state of such mortal fear, your endorphins came to your rescue. You can't actually believe . . .

EVE. But we experienced the exact same thing.

MICHELLE. Your mother?

EVE. Yes, even she.

MICHELLE. That's good.

EVE. Odd, she popped into my head. How we all used to sing . . .

MICHELLE. Now that you are about to give birth, I suppose.

EVE. . . . before The Deluge. Mostly, I was thrilled for Opa. I'd never seen him as happy, as if everything he's fought for . . .

MICHELLE. Pie in the sky when you die.

EVE. Don't make fun.

MICHELLE. I'm not because at the same time, roughly, give or take, I began to experience the worst pains of my life. We knew I would need a C-section, as will you . . .

EVE. Not if I can help it.

MICHELLE. You will. You can see how they are, sharp little hooves and all. I did not want them stuck in the birth canal. If I could operate on myself, there would be a chance they would survive. You would come, or not, but two of them would be out. An animal would find them and raise them. A wolf-mother . . .

EVE. Your endorphins, likewise, kicked in.

MICHELLE. That was the story I told myself. I also began to feel exhilarated — there is no other word. I grabbed hold of a very sharp scalpel.

EVE. We found you collapsed, cut open. One was out, wiggling on the ground. One was stuck, but hoof-hand and face were visible. They were breathing. You were, too, barely.

MICHELLE. I could have lifted it out. I was coming back awake.

EVE. No doubt you could have.

MICHELLE. I would have reached inside.

EVE. Sure. You could have bled to death, my darling.

MICHELLE. But they would have survived.

EVE. They did. So did you.

MICHELLE. I used spider webs to staunch the blood. I had gathered them from the woods. There are spiders here weaving webs. It felt criminal to rip them down, but I could think of nothing else.

EVE. You knew you would operate on yourself?

MICHELLE. I thought that I might once Tanaka left. I arranged my things. They worked, the webs, better than stitches I think.

EVE. My darling. You were so brave.

MICHELLE. Labor started, then stopped. I could no longer feel them move.

EVE. You risked your own life. That's what I can't forgive you for.

MICHELLE. [*Laughs.*] "My life."

EVE. You'll have quite a scar.

MICHELLE. You almost died.

EVE. It's difficult to say. It was like being swept up in music, going into a song.

MICHELLE. But Tanaka came, and here we are.

EVE. Can I lie down? I'm very tired.

[*Eve lies down in the bed with Michelle, kisses her.*]

EVE. Did you have sex with Tanaka, Michelle?

MICHELLE. Rest. Who knows when your labor will start.

SCENE 17

[*Tanaka and Opa stand together in the clearing, each with a newbie at the breast. They are nursing.*]

OPA. Hmmmm.

TANAKA. It's lovely.

OPA. It is conducive to . . .

TANAKA. Thought.

OPA. Indeed, it is.

TANAKA. What are you . . .

OPA. Thinking of?

TANAKA. Yes.

OPA. You, I am thinking of.

TANAKA. Me.

OPA. Whom I don't actually know.

TANAKA. Who I am . . .

OPA. How you did . . .

TANAKA. The women could not at this moment. Michelle has lost too much blood.

OPA. She has nursed . . .

TANAKA. For bonding, for looking in their eyes, solely.

OPA. Soulfully.

TANAKA. The important part.

OPA. So, supplying the actual nutrients is left to us.

TANAKA. Quite simple really. It might have been figured out, if given priority, of course.

OPA. It was never given that.

TANAKA. You saw yourself, a simple series of shots.

OPA. Would history have been different, if?

TANAKA. History was meant to be as it was, so there is now.

OPA. You believe that?

TANAKA. I seldom say otherwise . . .

OPA. Than what you believe.

TANAKA. It is not conducive to thought.

OPA. I agree.

TANAKA. You operate on a standard quite like mine.

OPA. One must speak as one thinks.

TANAKA. Thought before speech.

OPA. One need not speak, but language is required in order to think.

TANAKA. You ask me who I am. Where I come from.

OPA. I would like to know.

TANAKA. You move to the other breast now.

OPA. Right.

[*Pause as they both shift the newbies.*]

TANAKA. One is used up; the other fills up.

OPA. Neat.

TANAKA. Evolution usually is.

OPA. Tell me, Tanaka, just what you thought you were doing, when you violated nature so.

TANAKA. We wished to pick up where evolution left off, where evolution would likely have gone.

OPA. And you knew the way?

TANAKA. You, also, said similar things.

OPA. I wanted democratic solutions, not engineered creatures. I advocated mutual respect, individual liberty, public interest in the public good.

[*Pause.*]

OPA. This is quite an extraordinary experience, actually.

TANAKA. You felt the rush when the milk came in?

OPA. A bit like an orgasm.

TANAKA. That is oxytocin, the empathy hormone, being released.

OPA. I see.

TANAKA. Inside their brains, neurons are growing because of you looking.

OPA. Your recipe requires human beings. [*Speaking to his newbie.*] There, there, here it is. [*To Tanaka.*] Lost the nipple.

TANAKA. It came to pass that most of the human race was traumatized.

OPA. The ability to think ought to have been enough.

TANAKA. Empathy was being lost.

OPA. There were forces at work, economic.

TANAKA. Nothing explains the actions of human beings over time but that some essential biological connection remained unmade.

OPA. And you believe in the quick, mechanistic fix.

TANAKA. You, the last humanist.

OPA. And you, what do you call yourself?

TANAKA. I call myself Tanaka.

OPA. Don't be smart. I am asking a rational question. How do you identify, explain, name what you believe you are doing?

TANAKA. It is not a matter of rational thinking; it is a matter of seeing. I saw what needed doing. Eve and Michelle were engaged in similar acts of seeing. Our energy fields connected us.

OPA. Sounds like blah, blah to me. [*Pause.*] This one's eyes are quite bright; it has a rather intelligent, inquisitive look. Don't you? It's true. You're a smarty, you are.

TANAKA. They will be wise.

OPA. I won't go that far.

TANAKA. Keep pouring yourself into them.

SCENE 18

[*Eve, very pregnant, comes upon an agitated Tanaka.*]

EVE. What's wrong, Tanaka?

TANAKA. I've been nursing the newbies with Opa.

EVE. And . . . ?

TANAKA. He made me question myself.

EVE. He has that way, I'm afraid.

TANAKA. It is why we wanted him with us.

EVE. You are upset.

TANAKA. The past . . .

EVE. Reared itself. [*Pause.*] Tanaka, what happened to you?

TANAKA. [*He turns away from her.*] I saw my family swept away in The Deluge, after the rains, in the winds, the floods, the water rushed. A little girl of three with the brightest, roundest, blackest eyes in the world. I was holding her hand. My wife, a woman of such intelligence and instinct, we often needed barely to speak. We read one another's minds. With our son in her arms, a fat, smiling baby, fed at the same breasts where I had often suckled myself. They were gone while I watched it. Was I trying to swim, was I . . . I do not know . . . I saw the water like a wall, a force I had never seen before . . . I must have let go.

EVE. Tanaka, I, I'm, I thought something like that, but, I'm so, so sorry.

TANAKA. Stop. Please. Many have seen what I did. Did what I . . . Many have lost everything. Most. Let go. But, there is worse. On the road, walking inland, walking uphill, staggering away from the sea, a woman, battered by branches, cut and scarred, sea weed stuck in her hair, asked if I might carry her child. She had a baby in her arms and she felt she could not go on. She wished to pass the child to me. Maybe I could carry it somewhere. I was walking. I was strong enough. I passed her. I acted as if I had not heard. Perhaps, she had not said anything at all. Perhaps, she had only looked and I saw as I used to see with my wife without words what was needed. I walked faster, as fast as I could walk, I walked away from her. I believe she sat down with her child to die as I walked past.

[*Silence.*]

TANAKA. Homo sapiens became narrow-minded and selfish. They grew to think only of their own selves. They became limited in their compassion. I wished to go on, mechanically walking, without wanting, I walked, I kept on walking. Saving myself. We cannot think ahead; we cannot stop ourselves from grasping. We are afraid of death; we walk away, we walk past the suffering of those not us. The suffering of others does not touch us as long as we walk. We refuse to look. Even without a future, even without a plan, I walked on and on. One day it came to me, something slight. I began for the first time in a long time to be able to hear my heart beat. I began to walk in tune with that. I thought, suddenly, it was not thought, it was feeling welling up, and I knew there will come a day, a time to come, when this ignorance will end, when the heart and the head will beat inside in unison, a thrum, thrum. It might not happen to us. I had given up on people. On myself I had given up. But I understood, there will come a different moment, a turning, in years, perhaps sooner than we dare to wish, when life reasserts itself, and there will come a new, a noble race of creatures who are capable of living fully, who want the best for others, who understand themselves as a part of, not apart from, who neither fear nor despise, who recognize, who bear their lives gladly, willingly, with restraint, and with joy welling up, and they will be happy and fearless, careful, generous, and kind.

EVE. Tanaka, yes. I believe that, too. I do.

TANAKA. They would be stopped in their tracks. They would never be able to walk away.

EVE. Anyone can understand why you did.

TANAKA. Not them. They would not understand. They could not physically do as I did. They would not have been able to move. They would take the child. Bear any burden. Would not think only of themselves. Would not live in fear. You need to give birth to the other two. If I could have done so, I would have. But this has fallen to you.

SCENE 19

[Eve, finally, is beginning to have some labor pains. A plank delivery table in the hut. It's all rudimentary. Michelle is at the table, readying things.]

EVE. Where's Tanaka?

MICHELLE. [*Without turning around.*] One of the newbies is sick. One of mine, obviously.

EVE. [*Begins to cry.*] I didn't want it to end like this.

MICHELLE. [*Without turning.*] Nothing is ending. You're having some babies. It's a beginning.

EVE. Tanaka is not here to help.

MICHELLE. I can handle it, darling.

[Eve goes to her and hugs her from behind, as well as she can because her belly is very large.]

EVE. My hero. Always, my strong, capable Mick.

MICHELLE. Yes, but let me think for a minute. Let me think.

EVE. You are not going to cut into me. [*Hands on belly, a pain.*] Whoo . . .

MICHELLE. Breathe. I know how; it won't hurt much.

EVE. Tanaka is nursing your children. You made love to him while I lay in a cave starving.

MICHELLE. You were singing.

EVE. What was it like?

MICHELLE. Nice, very nice. Gentle in fact.

EVE. How could you do such a thing? I've got your children inside of me.

MICHELLE. My DNA. Tanaka's too. Yours. Who knows who else?

EVE. Ours, our children.

MICHELLE. Not for long. Inside you, I mean.

EVE. Do you love yours?

MICHELLE. Tanaka certainly does.

EVE. You, I am asking you.

MICHELLE. Look, you can't tell until we get them out. I've seen it. I used to see it in the early days in The Dome when people were trying, pretending I suppose, to go on as normal, relieved. The woman you thought who had everything, bright, with a nice husband, would freeze, literally turn away when you put the infant on her chest. And someone else, in a far more difficult situation, perhaps, alone, without a companion, even about to be exiled, would yelp with delight, fall madly in love. Which child would end up with a better life?

EVE. The one with rich parents.

MICHELLE. Ha. That's what it came to, didn't it? That's why we're here, isn't it?

EVE. I suppose so.

MICHELLE. So, let's get them out and get on with it.

EVE. I think I'm a coward. I never thought so before.

MICHELLE. It's all right. We never do know. I'm going to cut you open.

EVE. No, you are not. I'm going to take a walk. One last walk outside. Think of that. I've hardly ever been outside my whole life.

MICHELLE. I'll come with you.

EVE. No, please, just a minute alone. You stay here and ready things.

[*Eve leaves. Then, a minute later, Michelle runs after her.*]

SCENE 20

[*Several hours later. Outside the hut. Tanaka waits. Michelle enters, extremely worried.*]

MICHELLE. Where is Eve, Tanaka?

TANAKA. I have not seen her.

MICHELLE. She went for a walk. She is afraid of a Cesarean.

TANAKA. I wished to perform the C-section last night; she convinced me to wait.

MICHELLE. So you let her escape.

TANAKA. I understood her wish to experience as much as she could.

MICHELLE. Eve always gets her own way — to do what exactly? To put her own life and all of our work at risk.

TANAKA. I understood her wish to know what her body could do. It seemed to me perfectly normal.

MICHELLE. That's a word that has no meaning.

[*Eve enters deep into labor, clinging to Opa who helps steady her. Her body convulses and she falls to all fours on the ground.*]

EVE. Stay away from her, from him.

MICHELLE. All right. She's back.

OPA. Help her, please.

MICHELLE. Get the equipment, Tanaka. Get the knife.

TANAKA. I must look. Hold her up.

EVE. I'm in labor, big one. It's natural. It's normal. It's [*she convulses in pain*] unbearable. I can't stand it. Help me, please.

OPA. Oh, my dear. Help her, Tanaka.

TANAKA. Breathe. You must breathe. Breathe with her, Michelle, Opa. I must discover.

MICHELLE. Look, we're going to cut them out, right now. Tanaka, please knock her out.

[*Tanaka is behind her, looking at Eve's vagina. He has his hand up her vagina, feeling.*]

EVE. [*Screams.*] Ouch. I can't do it. Stop.

OPA. Do something, please.

TANAKA. All right. You are fully dilated. You must push.

MICHELLE. What?

TANAKA. They are down too far in the birth canal for us to cut. Eve, you will be able to give them birth, but you must push. Let us try to straighten you up.

MICHELLE. Are you out of your mind? Cut them out. Right now. Or I will do it myself.

TANAKA. Stay where you are. Breathe with her, please.

EVE. They're down too far?

OPA. Oh, my dear, breathe.

[*He starts to breathe deeply.*]

TANAKA. They are in your birth canal.

EVE. I can do it? Oooheee.

TANAKA. Yes, Eve, you must.

EVE. Save them. I don't care. [*She grimaces.*] Cut me. Please.

TANAKA. Push, I tell you. Push, now.

MICHELLE. You don't care about your own life. You idiot, fool.

EVE. Sacrifice me.

TANAKA. Hold her, hold her up so that gravity . . .

[*Michelle takes over from Opa, holding Eve up, helping her squat. Opa begins to pace.*]

EVE. Are they going to come out? Oh, please, please, kill me, let them live.

OPA. My darling child.

[*Pacing, he cannot look.*]

MICHELLE. Shut up and push.

TANAKA. There are legs. This one is all legs.

MICHELLE. Fuck. Push.

TANAKA. I can grab the rump. Here, here, here . . .

EVE. Ooooh, oooh. I can't . . .

TANAKA. One more time.

MICHELLE. You can, you must. Push.

TANAKA. Here, here it is. I have nothing to wrap.

[*Opa stops, looks. He takes off his outer shirt and hands it to Tanaka who wraps the newbie. Opa takes the newbie and resumes pacing.*]

EVE. Help me, please. Aaaah.

MICHELLE. There are two of them, goddamn it, two. Where the fuck is the other little sucker. Let me strangle it and get it out.

EVE. I can't. I'm so tired. I cannot do . . .

OPA. Evie, my dear . . .

TANAKA. I can feel the head. Push. The child is here. I will pull.

MICHELLE. The child, he calls it.

OPA. [*Pacing*] It is something like that. [*Cooing*] Landed, you have, on earth.

MICHELLE. Pull its head off if you have to, just get it out.

EVE. Don't say that. How can. OOOawwoooo.

TANAKA. There. Here it is.

EVE. Two? Give them to me.

OPA. Wiggler, this one is. Look at that, hoof with toes, fingers, a thumb!

EVE. Good, that's good. Alert?

OPA. Eyes are closed.

EVE. Conscious, I meant?

TANAKA. Too early to tell.

OPA. Woke right up. Look at you looking out.

EVE. Let me, let me.

[*Opa gives Eve the newbie, bending over her, and they both look.*]

EVE. It's mama, baby.

OPA. In a manner of speaking.

EVE. Great-grandpa, too.

OPA. I suppose so.

EVE. Where's the other, Tanaka? Give.

[*Michelle sits behind Eve, holding her. Tanaka takes off his shirt and wraps the other newbie. He hands it to Eve.*]

EVE. Oh, look, look, look at them. Opa, look, what I've done. Hello, little ones. Oh, two, oh how precious, how sweet, my ones. Oh, how lovely, oh, my darlings, my dearest darlingest dears.

MICHELLE. Mother of the year.

EVE. Don't make fun of me, Michelle, just because . . .

TANAKA. Let us take them. Opa, please.

EVE. No. I want to hold them. Look. We will nurse. Oh, my sweetest, sweet, sweet, sweetest in all the world, bestest, you put your mommy through something, but we did it. We did. What loves, what loves they are. I feel so good. I feel like . . . Let me get up.

TANAKA. You feel no pain at all?

EVE. Pain?

TANAKA. We need to get out the afterbirth, but I feel, perhaps, you could go to a more sterile place.

EVE. I gave birth on the earth. On earth, I gave birth . . . to a new race.

MICHELLE. True to your name.

OPA. Evie, my child, you've done what you said.

EVE. They are beautiful, Opa, aren't they?

OPA. Interesting, I can say that. [*He takes one and holds it.*] Look at you, looking back.

EVE. Thought!

OPA. To be wished. Never mind. You're alive.

TANAKA. Let us get you up.

EVE. We give birth astride the earth, the light gleams. When we die we enter her womb. Decompose to be born again. Oh, Tanaka, if men could experience this . . .

[*Whimpers, then cries are heard.*]

MICHELLE. They're hungry again.

EVE. [*She laughs.*] Help me up. Let's go nurse. We will feed.

OPA. No worry, my child. I can handle things, now. [*He laughs.*] My milk is coming in.

MICHELLE. You might have died. You might have died and left me.

EVE. Oh, my darling, you were the one who almost died, who had no one, who cut yourself open, all alone. I had you, Tanaka, and Opa. I simply wanted to know.

SCENE 21

[*Several weeks later. Outside. Eve is holding her two newborn newbies, singing to them softly. Michelle enters with her empty bucket.*]

MICHELLE. Tanaka and I autopsied the . . .

EVE. Oh, Michelle . . .

MICHELLE. Don't "oh, Michelle" me. It had to be done. We buried it.

EVE. "It."

MICHELLE. What do you want me to say? We found nothing out. Of course, up here, wherever we are, we have nothing to work with, no real way to tissue test. Everything looked perfectly normal to the eye.

EVE. It must be so difficult.

MICHELLE. Stop.

EVE. Michelle.

MICHELLE. Don't.

EVE. What?

MICHELLE. Don't say "dear Michelle." Don't.

EVE. I won't.

MICHELLE. Good. Tanaka said a few words.

EVE. I wish I'd been . . .

MICHELLE. I couldn't have done it if you had been standing there, looking at me with pity.

EVE. I'm sorry.

MICHELLE. I could not have borne it.

EVE. Oh.

MICHELLE. Borne it, but I did. I bore it, and now I bear this.

EVE. Yes.

MICHELLE. It's the worst, the absolute worst. Losing a child. People say and you nod your head. They say, *"I never before knew what love was."* They say, they don't know how to go on. I've stood next to them. I've held their hands. They've wept on my shoulders. In another life. When there was that. Surgically clean environments, fluorescent lights. I've patted them on the back and walked away for coffee in the canteen, for a good laugh. I understood, I thought. I actually thought I understood. There is nothing worse than losing a child. But this, this has hit me so hard. It was mine; I bled on the ground for it.

EVE. Of course, my . . .

MICHELLE. Don't, don't talk. I cannot . . . I can't. I would have given it my life. I thought, if you and Tanaka never came back, those two, somehow, maybe a wolf would save them. There were stories like that from when life was, we used to have, and now, when we have so little, when we've lost so much, I, I just, I can't.

EVE. Michelle, let me . . .

MICHELLE. Don't come near me. Don't touch me. I don't deserve to be held. I don't want to be touched. I cannot bear your foolish kindness, your *empathy.* It's that that I cannot stand. Don't forgive me.

EVE. Forgive you?

MICHELLE. Yes, can't you see how tainted I am. How I brought it on myself; how I deserve everything I get. I drank.

EVE. Mick, you are hurting yourself more than . . .

MICHELLE. Than I deserve? It's not possible to hurt more, more than, more than I . . .

EVE. More than you hurt. I am so, so . . .

MICHELLE. No!

EVE. So full of love for you.

MICHELLE. Stop.

EVE. You did nothing wrong. It happened. These things happen. We can't understand. Even with instruments, tests, the results would likely be inconclusive. We don't know everything. Why some live. Why we lived. Why some give up. We can't, you know that, as a physician, you more than anyone, we cannot control anything. We ought not to have tried.

MICHELLE. What? Give up. We had to do something. Sometimes I imagine there are other bands out there, like us, doing things, birthing new ones, going on. And, now, this.

EVE. We have three left.

MICHELLE. I wanted, for a change, I wanted to have what everyone had. What was yours.

EVE. They are all ours; our genes are so mixed.

MICHELLE. It came from my body, from me.

EVE. Not "it"; did you name it? Tanaka must have when he said a few words. What did he call it, please?

MICHELLE. Surrender. That's what he said.

EVE. It's a beautiful name.

MICHELLE. Give up.

EVE. No, we won't. We will surrender Surrender. We will surrender him/her.

MICHELLE. I think he said Sunder.

EVE. Sunder. That's lovely.

MICHELLE. Sunder. As in, cut from me.

EVE. Yes.

MICHELLE. That is what it was.

[*Tanaka enters. He holds the surviving newbie of Michelle.*]

TANAKA. Sunder, I said.

[*They turn to him.*]

TANAKA. Leaving us sundered, un-limbed, torn. That is how it came to pass. They took everything from me. They used up the earth. And I vowed, not revenge, no, I vowed what we have done, a new species, a new kind. I thank you for your help. I thank you for your belief. I thank the three who have survived, and Sunder, too. I thank Sunder for showing us that we are still capable of grief.

SCENE 22

[*Some months later. Michelle, bringing food in, encounters Opa, pacing.*]

MICHELLE. I'm trying to stretch the soup; now they're eating so much. The foraging is thin. I've got a few roots, a wild onion.

OPA. Preparing my lesson plan. They are curious, smart.

MICHELLE. We will have to move north. It will be spring, heat and floods.

OPA. If I had books.

MICHELLE. You must have stories in your head.

OPA. How to tell of consciousness, self?

MICHELLE. In a rhyme.

OPA. I learned to read at age five from the titles of books that were scattered all about. *"How can there be Being and Nothingness at the same time?"* I was said to have asked my mother.

MICHELLE. How, indeed, Opa, how?

OPA. I shall teach them about Thoreau.

MICHELLE. I know how to implant, operate, not Thoreau.

OPA. On his deathbed, he said: *"I have loved nature so."*

MICHELLE. Mechanically useful, I've been.

OPA. I've lived in my head, useless to all but myself.

MICHELLE. I was never educated; all that had vanished. How to cut, slice, stick in my hand. Do whatever they wanted done. I fought my way into The Dome.

OPA. I'm sorry, I had no idea.

MICHELLE. Eve let me cry in her arms while she sang, while she quoted you, Opa.

OPA. *Gravity and Grace, Eros and Civilization, The Wretched of the Earth.* Even at five, I was fascinated.

MICHELLE. Your thoughts made me suddenly know one could forge a self, somewhere inside, outside their control.

OPA. People think, I thought to myself. They use language to tell what they know. I can think alongside. I carried whole worlds in my head.

MICHELLE. How will I feed all of us?

OPA. They follow me with bright eyes; nod their heads.

MICHELLE. They eat so much.

OPA. I cannot bear the thought thought might cease.

MICHELLE. I must put up the soup.

OPA. I must simplify, speak little, tell much . . .

[*He walks off, babbling to himself, making notes on bark with a quill.*]

MICHELLE. What I wouldn't give for a potato.

SCENE 23

[*Sometime later, outside. Michelle has been looking for everyone. Tanaka enters.*]

MICHELLE. Here you are, thank goodness. Where is everyone else?

TANAKA. Eve is with them.

[*Eve enters, breathless.*]

EVE. They've taken Opa. Kidnapped him.

MICHELLE. Impossible.

TANAKA. Miraculous growth spurt, programmed in.

MICHELLE. They were infants, babies a moment ago. Kids. They could do nothing for themselves.

EVE. It cannot have gone so fast. They cannot have grown up.

MICHELLE. They are children. They must be hiding. Opa must have set them up for a game. Hide and seek, that must be it.

EVE. His things were strewn about.

MICHELLE. What things does Opa have?

EVE. The bark he writes on. Shoes. He never leaves them behind. He stuffs bark into his pockets so he can jot things all the time. He does not go about in bare feet.

TANAKA. They've kidnapped him.

EVE. So I said.

TANAKA. They have free will. Proof.

MICHELLE. They are children, nevertheless.

TANAKA. They have to get on with it.

MICHELLE. With what?

EVE. Growing up.

MICHELLE. That's what we are here for, to parent and advise.

TANAKA. It's going to get too hot to survive.

MICHELLE. We'll have to go north, fast. We've done nothing to prepare. We were so occupied with raising them. Playing. Nursing, chasing, teaching. We'd best get to work.

TANAKA. Our bones are cracking. Our strength went into making milk.

MICHELLE. You're saying . . .

TANAKA. That's right.

EVE. We knew it, Mick. We did.

MICHELLE. It happened in an instant.

EVE. They grew up all of a sudden.

TANAKA. Had to, before the heat, drought.

MICHELLE. How will they live?

EVE. They have insulation against hot and cold.

MICHELLE. There might be fish, birds. They will migrate north. Forage.

TANAKA. They will know how to live, if we did our job.

EVE. They've taken Opa.

MICHELLE. Out of all of us, chosen him.

EVE. We chose him.

MICHELLE. Ungrateful creatures, not you or me.

EVE. No one runs away, into life, with their mother at their side.

MICHELLE. But Opa?

TANAKA. We gave them him. That was always the thought.

EVE. He won't survive.

MICHELLE. He can't. He's old.

EVE. I always thought Opa would be forever.

MICHELLE. What shall we do now?

EVE. Like a wise owl.

TANAKA. Do?

MICHELLE. We were all about them, for so long, all my life, all my thoughts, first to make them, birth them, mourn Sunder, let Sunder go, raise them. What do we do?

TANAKA. We ought to die before the heat. I don't want to suffocate.

EVE. I've read that it's fast.

MICHELLE. We could cannibalize one another. One of us would live longer.

EVE. Mick!

TANAKA. The poisons in our systems will do us in.

EVE. It's the lost nutrients we gave them in our milk.

MICHELLE. How noble is that.

EVE. Quite.

MICHELLE. They didn't even say goodbye.

TANAKA. What could they say?

EVE. I snuck out on my mother. Never visited when she had cancer.

MICHELLE. So, it's your karma.

EVE. You knew this all before.

MICHELLE. I never for a moment thought . . .

EVE. But why not?

MICHELLE. It all went so fast.

EVE. They were babies a minute ago. How did they grow up?

TANAKA. It was as it was.

MICHELLE. What is that supposed to mean?

TANAKA. I have no idea.

EVE. I thought you were a Buddhist.

TANAKA. And so?

MICHELLE. You should have answers.

EVE. You should say, give up attachment, illusion.

TANAKA. I should say, I'll stay with you till the end, if you stay with me.

MICHELLE. I will.

EVE. I will, too. [*Pause.*] We're dying, Mick.

MICHELLE. We'll be together again in your Over-Mind.

EVE. The Over-Mind doesn't care about you or me. We are losing one another. I am losing you.

MICHELLE. [*They kiss.*] Goodbye my love.

EVE. Tanaka, too. Michelle, go ahead. [*Mick and Tanaka embrace; Eve embraces both of them.*] Poor Opa. He'll die alone.

TANAKA. The newbies are with him.

EVE. The newbies need us to reach full potential.

MICHELLE. We must find them while we have the strength.

EVE. Bring them back.

TANAKA. Start again.

EVE. They're too young to be on their own.

MICHELLE. They can't have gotten very far with Opa in tow.

EVE. They are going to eat him alive!

MICHELLE. Why else would they snatch him!

TANAKA. Let's not jump to conclusions.

EVE. They are mindless, ruthless.

TANAKA. We don't know what they are.

MICHELLE. We'll find his bloody bones, gnawed.

EVE. It's my fault. All of it.

TANAKA. Stop that! Let's go.

MICHELLE. Rescue Opa.

SCENE 24

[In a fragile, new wood: The Newbies are asleep in a stand of tall grass. Opa is some distance away, sitting on a rock, watching over them. The Newbies stir. We cannot see them, merely flashes of light through the woods in front of Opa. The Newbies begin to dance and speak; Opa strains to take in the sight. As the Newbies question Opa, he begins his own transformation. He loses language as their questioning intensifies. As the Newbies arrive at a sense of how to live on earth, Opa completes his metamorphosis from wise man into bird of wisdom.]

NEWBIES. [*Softly, hesitantly.*] We are, we are we.

We are, we are we.

[*Louder, insistent.*]

What kind of creatures are we, Opa?

What kind of creatures shall we be?

OPA. Creatures you are, you are, you.

NEWBIES. Opa . . . tell us, please.

How do we live?

How do we live?

We are new and you are wise.

How do we survive on earth?

Opa, how, how, how?

We speak, we think, we can conceive.

We need to know how

To live, Opa? How, do we do

What's good, Opa, on earth,

Where we are now, Opa, how?

OPA. Evie, Tanaka, Mick?

NEWBIES. How, Opa, how?

OPA. Who? Who?

NEWBIES. Opa, yes. You must tell.

OPA. Who? Are you?

NEWBIES. Yes, Opa, yes,

What do you think

Opa, what?

What must you say to us?

OPA. You, you, you.

NEWBIES. Do we, do we do,

We do, too, we think we do.

Like you, Opa, just like you.

What should we think, Opa?

What, what? Think we, what?

Opa, you must know. You

Know, you know what thinking is

You do, Opa. How should we be?

OPA. Be, be.

NEWBIES. Yes, Opa, think, do, live

How do we do, Opa,

How do we do as you?

OPA. I who, I who, I, who, you who.

NEWBIES. Opa, what?

OPA. How do. How.

NEWBIES. What? What?

OPA. Who, who.

NEWBIES. Tell us, Opa, please,

What you are, what you think we ought to be?

How live, Opa, how?

OPA. How, how, who.

NEWBIES. Yes, yes, that's it, what,

What? Tell us please what

Thinking is, Opa?

How do we be on earth, this is, Opa, how?

OPA. Watch.

NEWBIES. We, Opa, we. Tell us, Opa, please.

Watch over us.

Guide us on our way, Opa, please.

Way we walk

Thinking is, to talk, to say

Tell us, Opa, please. What, what.

What are we, what, what we must

Do. How be? How live?

What think, what say?

Not to make a mess of this

Our only world, Opa,

Our only world. We need, Opa,

Your words. Yours.

How do we live, Opa, how, how, how?

With awareness and restraint.

Yes, Opa, yes?

Using what we can replace.

What do you think?

Watch over us, Opa.

With kindness and restraint.

With love, with love.

[*Opa completes his transformation — and begins to hoot.*]

OPA. I will dooo. Whoo,

You, you, you

Whooo, whoo, whooo.

[*The wise old owl flaps his wings as it is about to take off.*]

END

4 Blue Valiant

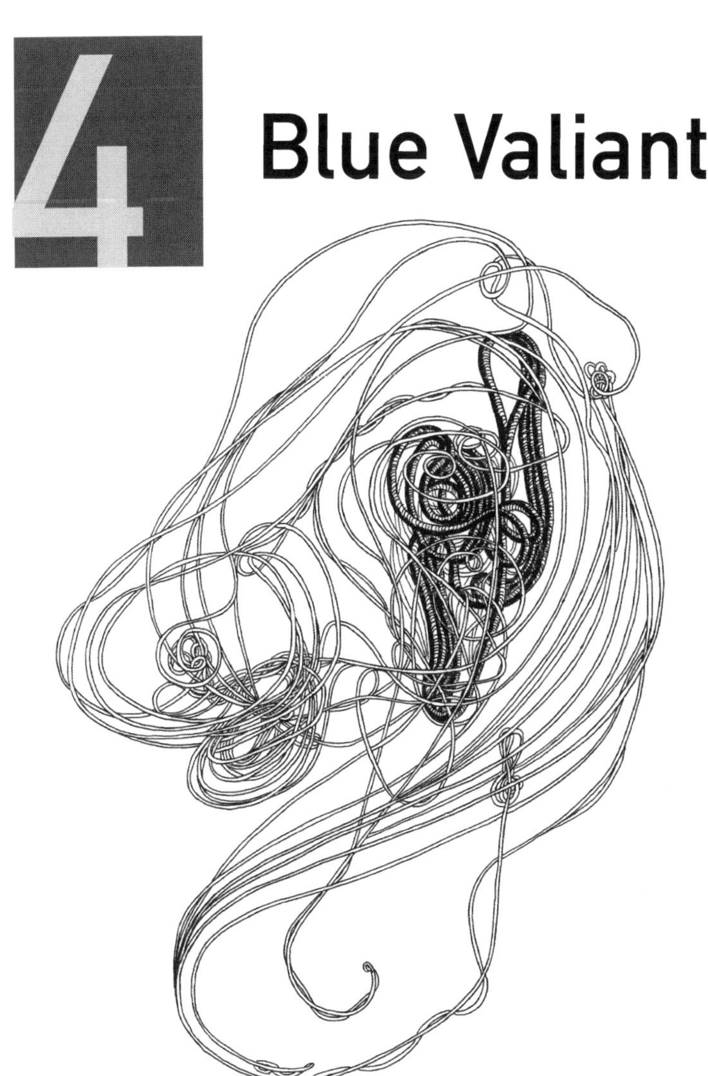

This play is dedicated to the memory of Candy Kid, a strawberry roan, and to the other horses who brought me through.

CHARACTERS

The horse, **BLUE VALIANT**, a blue roan, part Arabian, part thoroughbred, unusually beautiful, thick black mane and tail nearly to the ground, well-muscled, fine conformation, around 16 1/2 hands

HANNAH DOYLE, tough, wiry, attractive

SAM BROWN, an old horseman

MAYA ZELAYA, a 14-year-old immigrant from Honduras

SETTING

A recent summer at Sam's barn on Long Island

Staging notes: For the premiere production by Theater Three Collaborative at Farm Arts Collective, we staged the play along the greenhouse (which became the barn) wall. A 2' high, 8" square stage with Sam's chair was stage left, with steps up the right side and across the front. Blue Valiant, as a piano, played by Arthur Rosen, was on the ground, in the pasture farther stage left. The barn door was center stage. To stage right of the barn was Blue's stall and this is where the projections, when they came up, are seen. Farther right was a cot, representing Hannah's bed and breakfast room. Sam remained seated on the stage the entire time, like a minidivinity overlooking the action. Hannah's monologues took place on the downstage steps, as did Maya's.

SCENE I

[*Outside his barn, Sam Brown sits where he always sits. Hannah Doyle walks into scene. She is well dressed, in a light summer dress, flats, carries a purse.*]

HANNAH. Excuse me; is this barn yours?

SAM. Don't belong to no one else.

HANNAH. I see.

SAM. See what?

[*Pause.*]

HANNAH. I was driving by . . .

SAM. Without a care in the world.

HANNAH. Hardly.

SAM. Hmph [*as if he doesn't believe her*].

HANNAH. I saw the most beautiful horse, running free, in that large pasture over there.

SAM. You stopped your car.

HANNAH. I did.

SAM. Stopped in 'er tracks by the blue roan.

HANNAH. Such a magnificent horse.

SAM. You sit for a bit; then you git yourself out and amble up, close to the fence.

HANNAH. Not too close.

SAM. And the blue roan, what did he do?

HANNAH. He started galloping.

SAM. Right at the fence.

HANNAH. Fast as light.

SAM. Scared the daylights outta you.

HANNAH. I got back in the car, to find the owner.

SAM. Weekenders stop all the time.

HANNAH. It's hard not to stop.

SAM. Got to put up a sign. "Killer Horse. Do Not Get Out."

HANNAH. I can hardly believe . . .

SAM. Gone over that fence once or twice.

HANNAH. I would love to see that.

SAM. Cleared it clean.

HANNAH. Splendid.

SAM. Found his way back.

HANNAH. Good for him.

SAM. Highway all around.

HANNAH. Dangerous.

SAM. Raised it up. Crashed through. Threw his whole self.

HANNAH. My lord. Was he hurt?

SAM. Gash on his neck.

HANNAH. Oh, dear.

SAM. Let him break his neck clear.

HANNAH. You cannot mean that.

SAM. Canna?

HANNAH. No, or yes?

SAM. Reinforced the fence.

HANNAH. So, the horse belongs to you.

SAM. Horse has fallen into my care.

HANNAH. Who owns the horse?

SAM. Where you come from everything belongs to someone.

HANNAH. Not exactly.

SAM. Makes people think, "*if only . . .*"

HANNAH. I suppose so. I hardly know what I think . . .

SAM. These days.

HANNAH. These days, quite so.

SAM. Once you knew it all, did you?

[*Silence.*]

SAM. No more.

HANNAH. No more, yes.

SAM. Knowin' nothing at all, you were stopped by the blue roan.

HANNAH. I'd like to find out who owns him. Someone must.

SAM. Nobody owns that horse, Mrs.

HANNAH. Please, don't call me that.

SAM. Meant no disrespect.

HANNAH. I understand.

SAM. Got no one myself.

HANNAH. You have a horse.

SAM. That particular horse goin' straight to the feedlot come fall.

HANNAH. Don't be ridiculous. This is Long Island, after all.

SAM. Nothing more useless in this world than a gelding cannot be rode.

HANNAH. You wouldn't dare.

SAM. Put a bullet right through his skull, gits out one more time.

HANNAH. That's ghastly.

SAM. I ain't goin' to winter him through.

HANNAH. He's such a magnificent creature.

SAM. Lucky if I gets me a few hundred dollars by the pound.

HANNAH. Don't say such things.

SAM. You want to feed him?

HANNAH. It can't cost very much. You could bill me monthly, I suppose. I'll leave you my address. [*She fishes something from her purse, hands him a card.*]

SAM. [*He scrutinizes, reads.*] "Hannah Doyle, Public Relations Representative." [*Pause*] Who you represent, Hannah Doyle? Bad horses can't be rode?

HANNAH. I suppose I should get a new card.

SAM. Not relatin' to the public much?

HANNAH. Not recently, no.

SAM. Sam Brown, myself.

HANNAH. How do you do.

SAM. Simplest name 'n the whole world.

HANNAH. Well, in the English-speaking world, perhaps, yes. Sam Brown.

SAM. Easy to remember, or forget.

HANNAH. Not that Hannah Doyle is in any way memorable.

SAM. You "wish" to feed a doomed horse. I could remember that. Add you to the list.

HANNAH. If money is the issue.

SAM. Could have sold that horse a dozen times, if I wuz not an honest man.

HANNAH. He stops people at your fence.

SAM. He does that.

HANNAH. You simply wish to condemn him.

SAM. Be at the feedlot come the first frost.

HANNAH. You enjoy disposing of horses in that way.

SAM. Be rode or be disposed. How life is.

HANNAH. A beautiful creature like that.

SAM. Useless to all but hisself. Not much use to hisself at that.

HANNAH. Running free.

SAM. Drives hisself wild.

HANNAH. Arabian?

SAM. An' a fair piece of thoroughbred, I'd say.

HANNAH. What was he bred for?

SAM. Seein' how he cleared that fence…

HANNAH. Show jumping?

SAM. Knows a bit do you?

HANNAH. Used to.

SAM. He kin eat that grass till it's gone but I ain't gonna winter him through.

HANNAH. So you said, but I can't accept that.

SAM. Gelding can't be rode got no good use in this world.

HANNAH. You're repeating yourself.

SAM. You don' seem ta git the drift.

HANNAH. Repetition is a sure sign that you remain unconvinced.

SAM. Don't you go fallin' for him. Beauty is as beauty does. Killer that horse is.

HANNAH. No horse is a killer, Sam.

SAM. You go on over, near that fence, not too near, mind you. Check 'im out.

HANNAH. Surely not.

[*She walks off. Sounds of the horse, snorting, pawing, charging, rearing up, and banging against a fence. Hannah returns.*]

HANNAH. My lord.

SAM. City folks don't listen up.

HANNAH. He charged straight at me. He hit the fence, purposefully.

SAM. Told you so. Doing the same thing over and over agin is a sure sign of being thick in the head.

HANNAH. I've never known a horse to do that.

SAM. Does it to someone else, I'll not be waitin' for no frost ta put a bullet straight through 'is head.

HANNAH. Well, I can see why you feel that way.

SAM. Good. Now, you have a nice day.

HANNAH. How much will you sell him for?

SAM. Told you, I couldn't give that horse away. Wasn't so purty, he'd been dead already; you keep on talkin' and you'll convince me. Got a gun in the barn.

HANNAH. I don't want to listen to such talk. How did you come by this horse?

SAM. Now, that's a story, all right. I'm sittin' right here in this spot, overlookin' the work. A fancy trailer pulls up. Green and gold. The kind with curtains on the windows, screens. Fancy stable name on the side. A shamrock. Virginia plates. Driver hands me a roll of bills. Hundreds, every one. Ten thousand dollars. Tells me to open up that there pasture gate. Drives the truck in, opens up the back, runs to get back in the cab. Horse damn near falls out. Drugged near to death if I ever seen it. Kin barely stand; head hangin' low. Stays still for hours. Never seen nothing like that. Pretty as can be. Driver drives off. Not a word. "*Grief*," I says to myself, like I says to myself when I look at you.

HANNAH. You do?

SAM. Then he wakes up an' turns mean. Don't you do that, Hannah Doyle, when you wakes, I am warnin' you. But, I got ten thousand dollars in my hand. Figure I could sell him for that much or more, once he kin be rode. Damn-near prettiest horse I ever saw. Near broke my back just tryin' to get a bridle on him.

[*Silence.*]

HANNAH. I'd like to buy him from you. I'll keep him here, only until I can find somewhere else. Keep him right where he is, in that pasture, by himself, until he'll go into a stall. When it gets cold, I suppose.

SAM. That horse gonna catch his death in that field, like as not. He ain't gonna let you near 'im near no matter how much money you got.

HANNAH. Nevertheless, I would appreciate the opportunity to purchase the blue roan.

SAM. I'm an honest broker of horses. Folks 'round here appreciate that. They want a horse for their kid to show, they come to me. I don't overcharge.

HANNAH. Name your price.

SAM. Horse not worth nothing but by the pound.

HANNAH. You are not selling that magnificent creature for meat; you are not putting a bullet through his head. You are bluffing, in fact. You, Sam Brown, would not do that.

SAM. Done it when I had to, you kin bet. Like broke my heart more than once. Horse business is tough. They go down. Leg broke.

HANNAH. I'm offering to buy that blue roan from you for what he's worth.

SAM. He's a pretty thing, all right.

HANNAH. How much do you want?

SAM: [*Laughs.*] Drive a hard bargain, Hannah Doyle.

HANNAH. Is $5,000 enough?

SAM. Not for that horse.

HANNAH. A minute ago, you said he was worthless.

SAM. Not to someone who wants him, he's not.

HANNAH. $10,000 is as high as I'll go.

SAM. I got to keep him here, too. Can't be rode; sure as hell can't be moved. Can't no one get close.

HANNAH. I'll pay his monthly board. I want a large, warm stall, with a window.

SAM. Stall with a view. You got yourself one useless piece of meat. Pretty though.

HANNAH. Since we are agreed on the price. [*She opens her pocketbook and writes a check.*] Here you are. Deposit as soon as you wish. It's good. I just took the bastard for all he was worth.

SAM. A mean woman of means.

HANNAH. If you mean money, I suppose.

SAM. No sense talking sense to the rich.

HANNAH. I'm going to meet my horse.

[*Hannah exits to pasture, behind hay bales.*]

SAM. Don't you go getting close to the fence. [*To himself.*] One of them's met their match. Can't tell which. You're a foolish man Sam Brown, suckered in for $10,000, and now you got to watch. But what would Molly Brown have said if I come home penniless, after having shot that horse? What would you say, Molly, from the grave, now, that I finally got some good sense? That I'm stuck with Hannah Doyle and her no-good horse.

[*Blue is pawing, snorting, running. Hannah's voice. "Whoa. Whoa. Stop, right now. Stop! I tell you. Stop!" Horse whinnies loudly. Silence.*]

[*She comes back, holding one shoe in her hand.*]

SAM. Horse hit the fence.

HANNAH. Not quite.

SAM. Crashed through it once.

HANNAH. You've told me. I suppose I was lucky.

SAM. Hightailed it out of his way.

HANNAH. I did not. Stood my ground. Waved my arms. Lost my balance.

SAM. Afeerd.

HANNAH. He was running straight at me with a wild look in his eye.

SAM. What'd he do when you fell?

HANNAH. He stopped. I got up. We stood looking. He dropped his head. I walked away.

SAM. I'll call that a draw.

HANNAH. Is there a hotel, a motel, a bed and breakfast nearby?

SAM. Motel too seedy for you, Hannah Doyle. To the left as you go out. Bed and breakfast, fancy place, down the same road apiece.

HANNAH. Thank you, Sam Brown.

SAM. You sit a few horses, you said.

HANNAH. Many years ago.

SAM. Good?

HANNAH. I was good enough.

SAM. Ribbons to prove it?

HANNAH. Quite a few.

SAM. Hannah Doyle, mind if I ask, what happened to your life?

HANNAH. I'd rather not say.

SAM. Like the horse.

HANNAH. I suppose so, yes.

SAM. You buy a horse can't be rode 'cause you been broke inside.

HANNAH. And then?

SAM. It's a dangerous business. That's what it is. People kin die.

HANNAH. I suppose so.

SAM. Sometimes that don't matter much.

HANNAH. I suppose not.

SAM. He's a magnificent creature, like you say. Take my advice, drive by and look. I'll feed 'im for you.

HANNAH. I have paid you $10,000. I am going to ride that horse.

SAM. If riding is what you want to do, I've got some nice steady ones I could lend, for someone your age. We don't bounce as good as we did. Get a young 'un to sit that horse, not that anyone kin.

HANNAH. I'll see you tomorrow, Sam. After I've settled in. [*She exits.*]

SAM. And so, Molly Brown, that's how I came by this here ten grand. An honest but a foolish man. Isn't that what you'd say. Foolish, perhaps, but I didna relish putting down that damn fine horse.

[*Blue musical interlude.*]

SCENE 2

[The next morning. Hannah is looking quite smart in jodhpurs, expensive high boots, a tailored shirt, holding a bunch of carrots. Sam is seated in his usual spot.]

SAM. Very nice duds, Mrs. [*He corrects himself.*] Mzzz. Doyle, it now would be. Lookin' smart.

HANNAH. Good morning, Sam.

SAM. Top o' the morning ta you . . . Now, may I inquire what you are settin' ta do dressed as you are?

HANNAH. Take a look at my horse.

SAM. A look, that's all. You ain't figurin' to jump right on top a 'im?

HANNAH. We'll see.

SAM. An' break your neck. 'Cause that $10,000 you gave me ain't enough to clean up that mess.

HANNAH. Come, come, Sam. I am quite capable of taking care of myself.

SAM. Good luck to ya, then, Hannah Doyle. But let me says this as I've come to like you a bit. That horse pretty as can be is no damn good. Horse gone wrong. Like some men you mighta known.

HANNAH. Quite a few.

SAM. And what do you do?

HANNAH. Stay away.

SAM. That's right. Or git away fast if you git tangled up.

HANNAH. Fast as you can. [*She is thinking of her life.*]

SAM. That horse kin run fast, too, I'm tellin' you. No way to know what he's goin' ta do.

HANNAH. [*Dismissing him*] I appreciate your concern.

[*Hannah walks toward the pasture. As she approaches, Blue begins to snort and paw the earth.*]

SCENE 3

[*Hannah stands at the pasture fence.*]

HANNAH. Okay, my big, handsome guy, how about some carrots? After all that grass, I bet you'd like that, a carrot and a scratch. You've gotten yourself a bad reputation. Undeserved, in my estimation. A horse needs some company. Herd animals, you are. Social beings. If it can't be another horse, right now, it can be me. I need some company, too, as it turns out. I, too, am not certain what to do. [*Silence.*] My way fell away, fell out from under. [*Hannah clucks, holding the carrots over the fence.*] Come on, big guy.

[*Blue whinnies loudly.*]

HANNAH. Come on over, I'll rub your ears. You can munch and get scratched. You must have fly bites that need looking after, that forelock I can untangle. Come on, my boy.

[*Hannah steps behind the bales, out of sight, as if entering the pasture. Blue snorts, paws the ground, and then begins to run straight at the fence.*]

HANNAH. For God's sake, slow down. Stop. [*She begins waving her arms, but the horse does not stop. There is a fierce thud as he hits the fence. The horse makes a sound of distress.*]

HANNAH. What have you done to yourself? You ran straight at the fence. I am leaving. [*The horse snorts and runs at the fence again, hitting it.*]

HANNAH. Oh, Blue, how could you? [*Hannah starts back, mounting the steps.*] I used to say that to Em. Why do you want to hurt yourself so much? Could not watch. Could not believe, could not put into words . . .

[*The horse is running at the fence, again.*]

HANNAH. No! Not with me watching. You will not.

[*Hannah turns her back. A terrible crash as Blue hits the fence.*]

SCENE 4

[*Sam has been sitting, listening. Hannah goes towards him, unsettled.*]

HANNAH. And don't tell me, you told me so, Sam Brown.

SAM. Didna say a word, Hannah Doyle.

HANNAH. You know horses, Sam.

SAM. That's so.

HANNAH. So?

SAM. I can't tell you no more than you know.

HANNAH. But, why, Sam, do you suppose?

SAM. Horse ain't speakin' to me. Some do. This one is closed-mouthed. Come here drugged.

HANNAH. But, why?

SAM. I ain't cashed that check.

HANNAH. I can have it back.

SAM. Yep. I'd miss you a bit, but I ain't been doin' this for cash.

HANNAH. What would happen to the horse?

SAM. I told you what.

HANNAH. You wouldn't keep him on? I'd pay for his food.

SAM. Till he kills someone or hisself? You pay for that?

HANNAH. It's all right. The deal's off.

[*Sam reaches for his pocket as if to take out the check.*]

HANNAH. Keep the check. I was momentarily upset.

SAM. Horse bad. Why cain't you accept that?

HANNAH. There is no such thing as "just bad" — or maybe there is — just not that horse.

SAM. What you got to prove to yourself?

HANNAH. A great deal, in fact.

SAM. I seen it before. Got nothing 'gainst it, neither. Lost, find a horse that's got to be tamed. You'll tame yourself in the working. But not that horse, Hannah Doyle. He'd soon as kill you. I got some nice horses in this stable. You want to ride. You want to prove to yourself you still can do it, come on with me, I'll fix you up. Come on, Hannah Doyle, that's what you need, a good run through the woods.

HANNAH. Perhaps so.

SAM. Come on with me, then. Got a bay mare will toy with you till you come 'round an' sit still an' be clear in the head what you want 'er ta do. She's smarter than you.

HANNAH. Most horses are.

SAM. Now that is certainly true.

[*She goes into the barn.*]

[*Blue's music: We hear the sounds of a horse moving off, calm and centered, and from the pasture, the snorts of the blue roan, his feet galloping along the fence.*]

[*Later, after her ride, alone. She uses the downstage monologue space.*]

HANNAH. Sam was right.

The bay mare was very nice.

Bright with a smooth gait.

A soft mouth. For a short while

The blue roan cantered along.

I rode well enough;

I haven't lost my seat. I know what
To do on a horse. The body remembers
If the limbs don't work as well, no matter.
The horse knows you know what you knew,
And forgives.
The body of a horse is a deep well,
A pool of knowledge. Just what does
A horse know? Horses put up with us.
They have four feet, after all,
Planted on this earth. A horse is
Something like a tree, rooted here.
And for humans this is a lesson
We seldom learn. And a
Blessing humans seldom accept
Seldom stop bucking against
Whatever life serves up.
A horse has come to understand
People are unsettled inside while a
Horse is deep. A horse has roots
That reach into the earth,
Back into time. A horse carries
The person on its back,
Until the person forgets
That separateness, which is so

Utterly human, that fear.

The steady

Rhythm of four legs

Under her renders

Her whole.

SCENE 5

[*The next day. Hannah enters in her riding clothes.*]

SAM. Enjoy your ride?

HANNAH. Very much.

SAM. Want to ride that little mare, agin, today?

HANNAH. I think not. I think I'll go see my horse.

SAM. Wish you would think again, Hannah Doyle.

HANNAH. I was good on that mare, Sam.

SAM. That you were.

HANNAH. I want to ride the blue roan.

SAM. That horse canna be rode, not by you, me, not by no one else. I had a trainer out here. A so-called horse whisperer. He was yellin' and swearin' by the time he was through. Horse just got worse.

HANNAH. But I think what I'd like to do first is introduce him to the bay mare. For awhile, yesterday, as I rode out, he cantered quite calmly along the fence.

SAM. I ain't gonna let you do that.

HANNAH. Why ever not.

SAM. Can't put that bay mare in harm's way. I canna.

HANNAH. Horses need other horses, Sam.

SAM. That is so.

HANNAH. And she calmed the roan.

SAM. Outside the fence for a minute or two. You want to ride her agin, that's good. The ride's on me.

HANNAH. Thank you, Sam. I want to ride her around outside his pasture.

SAM. I'm tellin' ya, Hannah Doyle, you'll drive that roan wild.

HANNAH. I don't believe I will.

SAM. You keep that mare away from 'im. If he goes over that fence, he'll like kill ya both.

HANNAH. I'll be careful, Sam.

SAM. You bring that mare back in one piece, you hear.

[*Hannah goes into the barn. There is bay mare music as Hannah rides her around the pasture. Then there are the sounds of Blue rearing up once, then once more, and flinging himself over on his back. Silence. Hannah comes out of the barn. She is shaken. So is Sam. Neither has seen anything like that before.*]

HANNAH. [*Shaken*] He didn't hurt your mare, Sam.

SAM. Like ta kill hisself. Reared up. Threw hisself right over onto his back.

HANNAH. Have you ever seen anything like that before?

SAM. Nope. If you'd been on 'im you'd be crushed. I seen that once. Horse broke a man's back, spared hisself.

HANNAH. I wasn't on him. No one was.

SAM. True 'nuff.

HANNAH. He wasn't trying to hurt anyone else, only himself.

SAM. That makes you fall harder for 'im.

[*Silence.*]

HANNAH. I suppose it does.

SAM. Hannah Doyle, I'm askin' you one more time, give up this fool's mission. The bay mare's the horse for you.

You ain't gonna tame that roan. You'll get yourself hurt bad before you do that.

HANNAH. I'll see you tomorrow, Sam.

[*Blue's music.*]

SCENE 6

[*Hannah enters with carrots.*]

SAM. So, Hannah Doyle. What you got on your mind today?

HANNAH. He tried to kill himself, not us.

SAM. That he did.

HANNAH. He is asking for help.

SAM. He is askin' for a bullet through his head.

HANNAH. He's my horse. You stop that talk.

SAM. You're possessed.

HANNAH. You might say that.

SAM. I just did.

HANNAH. Yes, you did. Excuse me, Sam.

[*Sam shakes his head.*]

SAM. I'll be right here where you left me.

[*Sam sits. Hannah walks toward Blue in the pasture.*]

HANNAH. There you are, pretty fellow. How about a carrot? Not paying any attention today? Mind if I come in, just inside the fence. You can come grab a carrot from my hand. That's a good boy. Yes, what a nice stare. I'm right here. I'm not moving.

[*Silence. Then we hear the horse snort, whinny, and paw. Blue makes a run directly for Hannah and the fence,* "No, stop, stop, right now." *There is a loud thud.*]

[*Hannah approaches Sam, holding her left arm close to her body with right hand, obviously in pain.*]

SAM. Heard the crash. What you gone and done?

HANNAH. He was perfectly calm. He wasn't paying any attention at all.

SAM. So, you went inside that pasture. Didn't I tell you? Doesn't make no difference at all what I say.

HANNAH. He ran straight at me. He turned at the last minute. Slammed me with his shoulder into the fence.

SAM. He damn near killed you, could have done.

HANNAH. He did not kill me. He intentionally did not.

SAM. You one damn city-bred fool. You think life comes to you your way.

HANNAH. I was foolish. I grant you that.

SAM. A damn fool horse and a damn fool woman.

HANNAH. Now, you'll drive me to the hospital, Sam.

SAM. You think you know it all, don't you, Hannah Doyle, order everyone around.

HANNAH. Drive me to the hospital, please. You can take my car.

SAM. Hannah Doyle, I kin no longer drive. Got the shakes.

HANNAH. I cannot move my arm. I'm in considerable pain. I'll talk you through. Please, Sam.

[*She almost falls into him as he stands to catch her.*]

SAM. Done dislocated that shoulder, if not also broke it. That's painful, I'd say.

HANNAH. [*Clearly in a great deal of pain*] It was my fault.

SAM. Always is. They's dumb beasts. You got a head. You goin' to learn yourself ta stay away from that horse. He done killed someone else.

[*Hannah leans on Sam as they walk to the car.*]

SCENE 7

[*Hannah in a morphine haze, in a hospital bed, her arm taped.*]

HANNAH. Here I am, shot through with pain and
painkillers just like you. It's delicious, isn't it, Em.
What fun, losing one's mind.

[*She searches for the bottle in the bed and takes one or two.*]

"I heard an old religious man
But yesternight declare
That he had found a text to prove
That only God, my dear,
Could love you for yourself alone.
And not your yellow hair."
"*Mama sing it more*," she twirled,
Golden hair throwing sparks.
Laughing her high, golden laugh
Light shooting out. Em.
I believed you would be held in God's hands
Till the end of your days, shining
Like joy. *"Mama, look what I drew,*
A dancing horse, with an apple balanced on his nose."
"Top of my class, think of that. Mama, I won
The debate. I proved prison reform is
Needed now. Punishment does not fix."

"I think he likes me, too. He asked me to the prom.

When I said yes, he picked me up. He

Twirled me around, in the middle of lunch."

"Princeton, Mama, I choose. I'll study

International relations and sustainability,

Or economics and psychology.

I want to do everything. I'll go into

Law then the State Department. Politics, after that."

Golden hair shaking. *"Sometimes, I feel*

I can do anything." You can, love, anything

At all. If anyone can, it is you.

No pain, how nice it is. On a scale

Of one to ten, sweet oblivion. Who

Wouldn't wish a painless life for

Those they love. Easy as pie.

[*Hannah swallows another pill.*]

"I don't want to be like this, Mama.

I am going to stop." Most young people outgrow

Their addiction, with or without treatment.

One day, they just give it up. Wake up.

Go back to their lives. So I was told.

"I can stop, I can. I know I can. I was being

Foolish. I don't want you and Daddy to worry."

Em, you are going to rehab. Not back to school

Like this. You need help. *"Leave me alone.*

You don't trust me." I trust you, but. *"Stop!*

"I've been perfect for you all my life. Maybe I am

Not what you thought. Not who you want.

Maybe I am a fraud. I flunked chemistry.

I don't know. It was so easy just to stop,

I was free — for the first time in my life. I felt

Like me. I am not what you want."

Don't be golden, Em, not for me. Just be.

"Please. I'll be fine. I promise you.

I broke up with that crowd.

Wasting their lives. I passed every class."

Em, you never call me back.

"Because you're always on my back."

Let me hold you one more time.

Twirl you around, *"those great honey-colored*

Ramparts at your ear,

Love you for yourself alone,

And not your yellow hair."

And she had a meteoric rise

Assumed a role in drug policy for the city.

"It's because I know, I am able to empathize.

We need treatment centers. Public education.

Drug users are not criminals. Rehabilitation."

If she didn't answer her phone. I would start to shake.

"Why can't you just chill out."

"You call me five times a day."

"Cures don't exist. We cure ourselves."

[*Silence. Hannah opens the bottle of pills, pours out a handful. Makes as if to take them all, then drops them on the bed. She sits up.*]

Does it invalidate a life

When your daughter dies in a drug epidemic

While your husband pushes his private parts

Up against young women in elevators,

And they both deny it to your face. *"I'm not*

Using. Recreational drugs of a weekend,

Everyone does. Besides, I stopped. I don't do that

Anymore. I am employed in the field.

You always jump to the worst conclusion.

Always on my back.

Behind my back. Yammering."

"I have always treated the young women

At the network with absolute regard." "I deny

Each and every accusation." "I understand 'no,' yes, I do."

Epidemic of a different sort. Weak they were.

In my heart of hearts, I disdained them both, my

Loves. Who should I blame? The drug manufacturers,

The Sacklers? We have given to the same museums,

I at a far lower amount. My name is not

Plastered across the entrance with money

Made from pushing drugs. Blame the government that

Refused to regulate, to warn; the doctors with

Their pain industry, their lack of time to sit and

Talk. Fentanyl, the lethal, lucrative

Substance that all of a sudden comes laced into every street drug.

It comes round and round in the middle of the night

To blaming oneself. Who else?

[*Pause; she sits up straighter.*]

Em took me to lunch. We went out to celebrate

Three months clean, again, drug free, back to work

Halfway through her *salade Niçoise*, she started to shake.

She excused herself. She went to the ladies' room.

I found her in a stall. That's funny, isn't it? I can't get

The horse into a stall, he stands in a field

Pawing the earth, as if digging his grave.

I found her crumpled

Against the door in the corner stall.

"Mom, I'm sorry. I am so sorry. I promise you.

I took hardly anything." Em,

Let me take you home. I'll give you a bath,

Put you to bed. She was thirty-five. She

Would call her fiancé, she said. Him!
I snorted and pawed at the ground.
I'll call your father. *"Him!"* She grunted.
*"He's got his prick in some chick a quarter your age.
He's fucking me in his head."*
I'll call the police. *"Fine, get me a record, fired.
Ruin my life. Get out of my sight.
I can handle this.
I will take care of myself. I have friends. Experts, I know.
Just leave me alone."* The next time I saw her
She was dead. Overdose, slipped away in
The night. Intentional? There was fentanyl,
Said the lab report. I did, Em, I do,
Love you for yourself alone and not
Your yellow hair.
[*Pause. She becomes clearer headed.*]
[*Hannah rings for the nurse and says into the speaker:*]
Nurse, tell the doctor I am leaving here, today.
I shall convalesce at home. [*She laughs.*]
So-to-speak.
[*Hannah leaves the hospital.*]

SCENE 8

[Sam enters and sits. Hannah enters from the hospital. She is dressed in riding clothes. Her left arm is in a sling. In her right hand, she holds a long pole with a long, thin rope attached.]

SAM. Look at you.

HANNAH. Wounded but not brought down.

SAM. Two men come to my barn while you wuz gone.

HANNAH. Very good.

SAM. Put up a chute from the pasture to that stall with a window you have rented.

HANNAH. Correct.

SAM. You, with one arm.

HANNAH. The work goes on.

SAM. You're something, Hannah Doyle.

HANNAH. Thank you, Sam Brown.

SAM. I ain't drivin' you ta no hospital again.

HANNAH. How's the roan?

SAM. Usual crazy self. Worse.

HANNAH. Misses me.

SAM. Couldn't say. Wouldn't count on it, though. What's that in your good hand, Hannah Doyle?

HANNAH. Horse-training equipment.

SAM. Hope you didn't spend too much. Enroll in some sort of crazy program.

HANNAH. I learned some things about the horse.

SAM. Stay away from him, I'd say.

HANNAH. He's not the killer you think.

SAM. No?

HANNAH. He has his reasons for what he does.

SAM. Someone whupped the daylights outta him.

HANNAH. How do you know that?

SAM. Usual story when you cain't get near them. Lots of mean sons of bitches in the horse business.

HANNAH. If he's worse, it's because he began to trust.

SAM. Liked ta kill ya.

HANNAH. He might have killed me, but he chose not to do so. I had pushed him too fast. He reacted with fear. Then I disappeared. Now, he thinks he might have killed me, too.

SAM. Thinks Hannah Doyle. You think too much; he don't think at all. You want ta think? Think about staying in one piece.

HANNAH. Thank you, Sam. That has been very much on my mind. The more I am hurt by him, the more hurt he becomes.

SAM. He's a dangerous beast. Horses are. Women go sentimental all the time.

HANNAH. To the contrary, Sam. Lying on my back, I became quite rational. I had time to search the web. Order my thoughts. Find things out about the horse.

SAM. So you got yourself a plastic stick with a string.

HANNAH. That, too. Now, I'm going to get my horse into the chute.

SAM. You ain't gonna git that horse inta no chute all alone.

HANNAH. You'll help me, I thought.

SAM. Did you, now?

HANNAH. Come on, Sam.

[*They go off toward the horse. They walk behind him. Hannah can use the pole at his feet to direct him. Blue enters the chute without trouble. An image of Blue's head fills the stage right side of the greenhouse/barn.*]

HANNAH. [*In a whisper, as she can hardly believe her good luck.*] Look at that. Walked right in. Thank you, Sam. I can work with him, now.

[*Sam goes back to his chair and sits. Hannah uses the flexible pole with string to stroke the horse's back, getting him used to touch. Blue is unsettled, pawing, snorting, but then, slowly through this speech, he quiets down.*]

HANNAH. Hush, now, hush. Something's

Touching you, yes. You are not untouchable, Blue.

Not anymore. Soon enough, someone, a hand

On your neck. I see who you are.

You've been found out. Quiet, now,

Pretty fellow, hush. Stand here, held by the chute.

Inside your stall, you have hay and oats.

Give a sniff. Maybe, later, you will want to go in.

[*She can leave the horse, now, for this inner monologue.*]

Because the animal does not speak, it

Is sacrilege perhaps to say what they know

Yet no one who has loved a horse would

Say they know nothing of what is on that

Horse's mind. How much we know might
Have to do with how close we dare come.
Once the roan quieted down, he could tell
Me about Sallie. How he came out all wrong,
When he was born, killing his mother. There was
That. No use telling him it was not his fault,
All legs he was, and the old brood mare died. Perhaps
She should not have been bred this one last time
But her foals were prized, and she mothered them.
So they bred her one more time.
It was Sallie who dried him off with a rough towel,
As much like a mare's thick tongue as could be. Still a child,
Sallie fed him with a bottle, pulled him to her chest,
Picked him up to his four feet, held the bottle just out
Of his reach, so he'd have to stay standing up
On wobbly legs. Even, then, she could see his
Astonishing beauty, the deep mottled black-blue
Of his coat, his bright eyes, the depth of his feeling.
Sallie mothered him; and he, in his way, mothered her.
She trained him as he grew until he followed her
Without a lunge line, without a halter, doing
Her bidding which was his, pleasing each other.
Like lovers.
And she, too, grew. She was so slight he barely

Knew she was on his back; her hands were so light
He barely knew there was a snaffle in his mouth
Her voice was so soft it was like the rustling of leaves
Or wind singing in the grass. She was quite simply
Part of him. He heard her step, smelled her smells
Before she ever said anything. *"Hi, my boy,"* was
How she greeted him and she rubbed his nose, stroked
His ears. She rubbed underneath his tail. She fell
Into him; sometimes, she'd be crying
But about what? She would stand next to his withers
Pressing her whole body into him, her hands around
Him, her face buried in his neck. He would turn
His head, he would nuzzle her, make low
Soothing sounds until she calmed. She would laugh
Then and toss her head. *"Let's go,"* she'd say. Sometimes
Without a saddle or a bridle, just a halter, nothing
On his back but her, so light, like a leaf,
Like a feather. They would run together.
She would lie flat, her arms loose, no reins
Nothing to hold him back. They would run
Like the wind in the night under the moon.
As if they were meant to be always slipped into life
Together, like this. So, I spoke to the roan,
Rubbing him all over with the pole while

Echoing his insides until he stood calm

In the chute, his ears perked, his breath even

For the first time in a long time.

Understanding, too, is a word we don't use,

Yet we know they understand, we can feel

When understanding comes, wordless,

A palpable thing, acceptance, trust.

Listening was just the beginning.

Okay, now, I am going to let you stand here in the chute.

I need some dinner. The hard part is over.

[*But the minute Hannah walks away, Blue begins to kick, buck, and snort against the chute. Oversize image of kicking horse.*]

HANNAH. Oh, damn.

SAM. Keeps up like that, he'll break his leg. Goin to dinner?

HANNAH. Of course not.

SAM. Keeps gettin' worse. You hear what I say.

HANNAH. Break a leg. Yes.

SAM. Let him go back to pasture.

HANNAH. I don't think so.

SAM. I'm goin' inside my own house. I'm no use. Can't stand the sound, as a matter of fact. When that leg breaks come and git me up. I'll bring the gun.

HANNAH. Before you go, just one thing.

SAM. What you want I kin give?

HANNAH. Help me get him into his stall.

SAM. Turn him out, told ya. Least he's not gonna kill hisself so soon.

HANNAH. Lose everything, no thanks.

SAM. Useless as it's been.

HANNAH. I don't think so. [*Pause.*] If I put him back out, it's over, Sam. I've lost and he's won — and you'll sell him to the feedlot as promised. Only, you don't want to do that. And you damn sure don't want to put a bullet through his head. He can't stay in the chute. So, go open that stall door.

[*Sam grunts but gets up and goes with her into the barn. The kicking continues.*]

SAM. Don't you go inside that stall. You hear what I say! He'd like ta kill you.

[*Sound of more kicking.*]

SCENE 9

[*Blue paces the stall. Then, exhausted, he lies down. Image of the big horse lying down.*]

HANNAH. Look at you, circling your stall.
Lying down in fresh straw. Miracle.
How exhausted you are. All that fuss. Quiet at last.
Now, my boy. There are things you need to hear, things I
Need to say. By tomorrow, if you cannot get up and walk
With me on a lead into the ring, and lunge, then Sam
Will have won. He can shoot you if he wishes, and I'll
Go home, whatever that means.
You think it's your fault. You
Think you missed the jump, your footing was off,
you started too soon, came down hard.
But Sallie was off her game. She trusted you
To carry her through, but she was barely able
To sit up straight. You didn't notice, or did you?
Did you decide to do it for her, win without her,
To compensate for her, as often I thought to do with Em.
Cover up, help her out, get her to treatment
On time? Sallie, too, had been prescribed OxyContin.
For the shoulder she injured when she fell
Off a colt she was training. Not you, off you

She never fell until . . . Maybe even then she was
Using. But you knew nothing of this. Your
Sallie with whom you had never made a false
step. Your Sallie fell off.
Not because of your stumble. You didn't
Stumble that much; you nicked the pole,
That's all. She might have righted herself.
You didn't go down. You regained your gait. But
Sallie was over your head and the way she fell,
The force. She broke her neck. She died.
You went right to her, everyone saw; the event is
Reported in some detail in the local newspaper.
As soon as you regained your balance, you
Went to the girl, gently, nearly kneeling at
Her side. You put your nose next to her face
Gently. You did not even nudge. Perhaps
It was clear to you right away, the life
Gone from the girl you knew so well. Others came,
The show doctor, the judge, and Sallie's
Father who had been watching from the
Stands; an ambulance was called, sirens
Screaming; "The horse stood motionless through
It all, never leaving her side for an instant."
Sallie's father grabbed the reins that were hanging

Over your head, in a fit of rage, "took up a
Whip and began beating the horse across his
Face, his neck, and his legs, fiercely
Ferociously, everyone gasped, and still the horse
Stood at her side, hardly acknowledging the whip."
It was written about in the local newspaper.
Until someone pulled the grief-stricken father back.
Then you let out a howl, that's what the newspaper said, a
Blood-curdling scream, not because of the whip,
But for her, everyone understood, for losing your Sallie.
I know, Blue, how that is, that sound we never
Knew we could make, up from the belly, up.
I have not touched anyone
Not since I yelled so for Em,
Could I bear anyone's touch.
[*Hannah goes toward pasture.*]

SCENE 10

[*Sam enters and sits in his usual chair. Late morning. Hannah with a long lead rope and a halter. Straw in her hair, slightly disheveled.*]

SAM. Ain't heard nothing.

HANNAH. That's good.

SAM. Where you been?

HANNAH. A walk in the woods, breakfast.

SAM. Got 'im up?

HANNAH. Oh, yes, before I left.

SAM. Now what?

HANNAH. I'm going to slip this halter on and take him out to lunge.

SAM. You think you is.

HANNAH. I bet I do.

SAM. Good luck, Hannah Doyle. I'll be right where I am seated right now. Ain't goin' to the hospital, no how.

HANNAH. I'll take that as a good omen.

[*Hannah goes into the barn, whistling. But the horse is pacing and as Hannah approaches, he begins kicking. Image of kicking horse.*]

HANNAH. Stop it.

[*Blue kicks harder.*]

HANNAH. Well, I'm not going to deal with this, no I am not. You will stay in your stall today. I need some rest. You need to get a hold of yourself. Good-bye, Blue.

[*The horse kicks harder, Hannah is almost crying.*]

HANNAH. Come on, fellow, stop it please.

[*Three quick, hard kicks. Snorts.*]

HANNAH. I can't, if I let you out, I'll never get you back.

[*She exits the barn. Image out.*]

SAM. I seen it once before in my life. A horse just askin' to be shot.

HANNAH. Shoot me, first.

SAM. You askin' for it, too. You want your heart broke agin; then you'll be no good for anyone.

HANNAH. I'm no good for anyone now.

SAM. Gave 'im a good try, you did.

HANNAH. I did. [*She drops lunge line and halter on the ground.*]

SAM. Some canna be saved, Hannah Doyle. An' if you're lookin' to 'im ta save you, I'd look somewhere else. You sit that bay mare very nice. Even at your age. She's a good horse.

HANNAH. I know that, Sam.

[*A volley of hard kicks. Hannah exits to B&B. Then quiet.*]

SCENE 11

[Early the next morning, before Sam has taken up his position, Hannah arrives with a few apples. It is silent.]

HANNAH. It's quiet; he's quiet. Don't let him be dead. Don't let him have hurt himself, please. Let him be standing quiet in his stall, his head hung. Let him be calm.

[Slowly, she approaches the stall, standing at the door. Still, no sound. She makes a few soft, hesitant clucks.]

HANNAH. Blue, my boy, Blue Valiant, that's what I'm calling you. In your former life, you were Knight Valiant the Bold, that seems a bit much; but that's done isn't it. Sallie's gone, my love. She wouldn't want you to die because she did. She knew it wasn't your fault. Did Em, I wonder, know that much? *"It's not your fault,"* she used to scream, except when she said once or twice, *"it's because of you. This house."*

[Silence.]

HANNAH. Come my blue boy. Blue Valiant. Good fellow. Look what I've got. Here's an apple. *[The horse makes some sounds.]* That's my good Blue, very calm. You bit that apple right through. Dropped half on the ground.

[Image of the calm horse's head. A girl, about 14, dirty, clutching half of the apple emerges from the stall and runs up the steps of the stage; she is very hungry and can't help herself, she takes another bite. She eats that apple throughout the scene. She is terrified to have been caught, and tries to ingratiate herself, to plead, to pray, beg for work.]

HANNAH. What are you doing there? Speak.

MAYA. Èl es un caballo magnìfico.

HANNAH. Yes, he is. Magnìfico horse. What were you doing in his stall?

[*Maya eats and cowers.*]

HANNAH. I see. Hungry.

MAYA. Por favor no me mande de regresso.[1]

HANNAH. As a favor? No, what?

MAYA. Pleese, no. Mi, en Estados Unidos.[2]

[*Silence.*]

HANNAH. I see. Guatemala? [*silence*]; Salvador? [*silence*]; Honduras?

[*She nods her head. She is agitated. She moves away.*]

MAYA. *Trabajarè. Trabajarè para ti. Lo que quieras, lo harè.*[3]

HANNAH. *Trabajarè?* Work, work for me? [*She mimes mucking out the stall.*]

MAYA. *Sì, Sì Mama. Por favor.* Pleese.

HANNAH. How long have you been here? What are you doing in his stall? He's a dangerous animal. Don't you know that? Bad, a bad horse.

MAYA. No, no. *Èl es un caballo magnìfico.* Pleese, Mrs.

HANNAH. Hannah can you say? *Mi nombre es Hannah.* My Spanish is rudimentary. [*She thinks.*] *Es su nombre es?*

MAYA. Maya.

HANNAH. Maya, very nice.

MAYA. Maya Zelaya.

HANNAH. Alliterative. Lovely.

1. Please do not send me back.

2. I am in the United States.

3. Work. Work for you. Whatever you want, I will do.

MAYA. *Sì. Trabajarè. Gracias.* Mama Hannah.

HANNAH. No, not that. Please. Go on home; I have to work with my horse.

[*Blue gives a low whinny.*]

MAYA. *Por favor no me mande de regresso.* Pleese *Senora* Hannah.

HANNAH. You're a quick learner, you are.

MAYA. *No me mande de regresso.*

HANNAH. I see. No. I am not going to send you back. You can stop worrying about that. How could I. With what is going on in this country and in yours? I may be self-involved, but I'm aware. Breakfast might be a better idea. After all, I suppose you tamed my horse.

[*Maya gets down on her knees.*]

MAYA. Pleese. *No me mande de regresso.*

HANNAH. Come, come, get up. In this barn we are all displaced. [*She offers her hand. Maya takes it and stands. They stand holding hands.*] Wait till Sam sees you. As a matter of fact, that better wait. I've no idea what Sam . . . You like my horse?

MAYA. *Èl es un caballo magnìfico. Sì. Trabajarè para ti.*

HANNAH. *Magnìfico,* yes, I think so myself. There are two of us. Three, including Blue. He is quite vain. You think so, too, don't you, Blue? He let you sleep with him. [*She mimes sleeping.*]

MAYA. *Sì.*

HANNAH. And eat half his apple.

MAYA. *Èl es un caballo magnìfico.*

HANNAH. That he is. But we were speaking of you. Where do you live? Where are your parents? Mama? Papa?

[*Maya shakes her head "no."*]

HANNAH. No? Nowhere? Here. [*She gestures to the stall; Maya cowers a bit.*] How long have you been sleeping here? You weren't here the other night. Were you hiding somewhere? Is that right?

[*Silence.*]

HANNAH. Why isn't it required to learn Spanish? How can one get along without it? Okay, Maya Zelaya from Honduras, resident in my horse Blue Valiant's stall, friend, so it appears to him; his only other friend. But that's good. He's no longer as wild as he was when I left him, unapproachable. He has found himself a girl. Am I superfluous once more?

[*Maya gets down on her knees, her hands held as if to pray.*]

MAYA. *Por amor de diòs.*

HANNAH. Sure, we all know what that means . . .

MAYA. *No me mande de regresso,* pleese, pleese.

HANNAH. Calm down. Calma. Calm. You are safe — for a while, at least, until I figure things out. Yes, of course, I am just figuring things out. You can stay with me, of course. *Mi casa. Si. Avec moi.* Do you ride? In Honduras, *magnifico caballeos*? [*Blue snorts; Hannah laughs.*] We are ignoring you, yes. You are magnificent, it's true. I am ignoring you for the first time since we met. What if we try to work the horse, together, you and I? *Si?* You can be my *"assistant." Sì. Trabajarè.* Let's get this halter on him so we can take him out to the round pen. In fact, you can do it for me.

[*Hannah hands the halter to Maya.*]

HANNAH. Hold the piece of apple in your hand. Like this, see. Let him dip his head.

[*Maya goes into the stall. Hannah in the barn doorway looks at Blue and Maya in the stall. Blue moves a bit, snorts. Image of Blue's head with halter.*]

HANNAH. There, very good, let him drop his head to you. That's right, rub his ear a little bit. He likes that. He likes you, I can see. Well, he let you sleep with him, didn't he? He likes you far better than he likes me. Well, I suppose I cannot complain. You remind him of Sallie, I suppose. You don't remind me of Em. I think that's good. Em is everywhere, anyway. I feel her eyes. It's difficult to explain. I've never said it before to anyone but to a girl who doesn't know English and a horse. She's always there asking for what I can't give. Come on, let's see if you can lead this horse. Hold the lead rope, just a bit loose. I'm right here, right next to you both.

[*The sounds of the horse leaving the barn. Sounds from the round pen. Image of horse cantering on lunge line.*]

[*Later, Hannah, in the woods, alone.*]

HANNAH. I took the lunge and clucked him into a trot.

We laughed with delight. Blue tossed his head

And broke into a canter. Amazing how it all comes back.

How beautiful he was. No wonder, we resist.

It's like a slap of happiness. *"Mi Blue,"* Maya cried.

She couldn't continue to sleep with the horse. She

Sleeps on a cot next to my bed, where she has peed more

Than once. Wet sheets are a small price to pay for the sound

Of her breath going in and out. She tells me her story

In the night, in the little Spanish I know and am learning,

In her bits of English. Like Blue, she tells me by the

Way her body goes stiff, high sounds, eyes wild.

She had come here with her father. *"Mi papi."*

They had left behind her mother with two younger

Children. Her father would find work. She would go

To school. *"Yo quiero estudiar,"* she says. She wants

To learn. But, at the border, they were stopped.

Her father was taken from her. *"Se llevaron a mi papi."*

They put her in a cold place with many children.

"Algunos de ellos bebes."[4] Babies, I said. *Si.* Mz. Hannah.

"Si, bebes sin madres."[5] *She rocked them back and forth.*

They cried together. Then, suddenly, she was put

with some other children on an airplane.

"Nos pusieron en un avion." She got to speak to her

father on the phone. He told her to be a good girl.

To stay here. They were going to give her a new family.

She cried. "No quiero una neuva familia, Papi."[6]

"You will study, you will learn, you will make me proud.

I will come back, someday, with your mother, your brothers."

"No nos olvides." Don't forget us, he said. She promised him.

No one forgets anything.

[*Maya emerges from barn, dressed for riding.*]

HANNAH. But how did you get here, to his stall?

4. Some of them were babies.

5. Yes babies, without mothers.

6. I don't want a new family, Papa.

[*Maya walks into the scene.*]

MAYA. Me escape.

HANNAH. I see.

MAYA. *El caballo, yo sabìa del caballo. Un caballo magnìfico.*[7] Blue Valiant.

HANNAH. Yes. He is. There is something also valiant about you. *Magnìfico,* too.

[*Hannah and Maya walk toward B&B. Sam speaks from his chair.*]

SAM. Me, I ain't gonna say nothing, till something is said. She brings that girl-child in the back way like I don't see. I don't say. Ain't none of my business, after all. The horse is going along, just fine. Damn thing is near training hisself. 'Course he knew it all before. Got hisself a girl. Damndest thing I ever saw. That's what was needed all along. Girl child, who coulda guessed it? But I don' say, nothin' and neither does she. We nod to each other. Can't hide her forever.

[*Hannah and Maya enter.*]

HANNAH. This is Maya, my granddaughter, Sam.

SAM. She ain't no grankid a yourn.

HANNAH. She most certainly is.

SAM. I know the sheriff you know.

HANNAH. How delightful. I'd love to meet him one day.

SAM. I kin call him over at any time.

HANNAH. That's so very comforting.

SAM. So, Hannah Doyle, you got yourself a grankid and a horse.

7. I know this horse. He's a magnificent horse.

HANNAH. That I have.

SAM. Reckon I played some small part.

HANNAH. Reckon you have.

SAM. She gonna ride that horse.

HANNAH. She is.

SAM. Horse gone an' got hisself a girl child.

HANNAH. Has.

SAM. So all's right with the world.

HANNAH. Wouldn't go that far.

SAM. But things is better than they wuz.

HANNAH. Indeed, they are.

[*Days later, early morning. Sam is already seated in his spot. Horse music. Image: Maya has fallen from the horse. Blue hangs his head, sad. Hannah enters.*]

SAM. That gal o' yourn come by early.

HANNAH. She wanted to talk to Blue. She promised me she would not ride.

SAM. Ought to know a horse-struck gal ain't gonna do what she says.

HANNAH. She was crying all night, Sam. Quietly, thinking I would not hear. What was I supposed to do?

SAM. Got throwed hard.

HANNAH. My lord.

SAM. Bounced like they do at her age.

HANNAH. Oh, to be young again.

SAM. That horse ain't never gonna be good.

HANNAH. You are forever the voice of doom.

SAM. You kin let her sit him a bit. On the lunge. He'll try. You done brought him that far.

HANNAH. What happened with Maya, Sam?

SAM. They was fine, out in the pasture, bareback, she had him going nice an' slow. Pretty sight, I say to myself, but I knew.

HANNAH. What did you know?

SAM. Horse canna not-forget. They forgives, that's far as they get. You might say, that horse has forgiven you and the gal, an' himself, some.

HANNAH. And so?

SAM. There's a long memory inside a horse, is all. Somethin' gonna rear up. He ain't gonna be able to stop. You might know when, but that gal, she's too young. She canna know how things come like rockets outta the mind. I'll sell you the bay mare. Good, trusty horse for her.

HANNAH. I see.

SAM: A hurt horse is predictable, they say, but ain't never gonna be reliable. How's that for some big words, now?

HANNAH. I'm impressed.

SAM. You kin think 'bout what they mean. Maybe you knows yourself.

HANNAH. You're reliably unpredictable, Sam.

SAM. We've arrived to some understanding, then.

[*Hannah walks toward the stall but stops when she sees Maya sitting outside crying. Her head buried in her legs. She is moaning a bit, crying.*]

MAYA. *Mi Papi, diòs mio, Mi Papi.*

[*Inside the stall, Blue also seems to be in distress. He is making low sounds, like moans.*]

MAYA. [*Slowly raising her head*] *Mi Blue, mi caballo.*

[*Maya sits outside Blue's stall.*]

MAYA. Ssshhh, *mi caballo,* ssshhh.

[*From inside the stall, the low moans of the horse.*]

[*Hannah approaches but stops, unseen, by Maya to listen.*]

MAYA. Hush, hush. I will talk English, Blue. This is what you talk. So, I try. We do not tell Hannah I fell off. You threw me. If Sam saw, I hope not. You spook. You jump. But I did not sit right, thinking only of you. *Vi a mi papá mirándonos. Que feliz. Que feliz,* I was with *mi papi.* Look, *Papi, esta es mi Blue, Papi. Mi caballo!*[8]

[*Blue snorts.*]

When you . . . Why Blue you jump? *Pensando en qué?*[9] Inside, what comes out? *Te agarra, qué?*[10] *Mi papi,* grabbed me. Who, you? You jump. I fall. Who grabbed you, *mi* Blue?

[*Blue nickers.*]

MAYA. I can be here with you, here, but I cannot be there. You cannot be with me. It comes up. I cry. You jump. I have no way to say.

[*Blue paws the stall and nickers more loudly.*]

MAYA. *Sì, sì tranquilo*, hush. *Tranquilo.* Stand. [*The horse quiets.*] Good, good Blue. We will try hard. We will not be. You, me. Ever like when, when *mi papi* lifts me up, tosses me on

8. I saw my *papi* looking at us. So happy. So happy. I was with him. Look, *Papi*, this is my Blue, *Papi.* My horse.

9. What were you thinking?

10. Who grabbed you?

the back of *el caballo huesudo,* not *muy magnìfico, flaco, sarnoso* [11] all over him . . . We will not say to Hannah, *nunca.* I did not fall off you. You did not spook. Hannah no, no, ever, those things we do; we *nunca* say. *Mi* Blue boy.

[*Blue makes contented sounds, so does Maya. Nor will Hannah ever tell she overheard.*]

HANNAH. Maya, are you in the stall? Let's clean him up. We'll lunge him today, no ride.

MAYA. I want up, pleese, Mz. Hannah. He will say he is bad if I do not. Pleese, Mz. Hannah.

HANNAH. All right, but on the lunge line. And then, we will phone your father after we are done. You can tell him all about Blue. After that, I have a bay mare I want you to ride.

END

11. A skinny horse, not magnificent, bony, with mange.

Dinner During Yemen

An Intervention

[Nita and Rita meet for dinner at Rita's house. They are friends from work, among the remaining career diplomats in the State Department. Nita is more knowledgeable in the ways of realpolitik than Rita, who looks up to her. There is no need for realist props. In the first performance, the actors stood, with wine glasses in their hands.]

[A terrible cry is heard.]

NITA. Is that an animal?

RITA. Or a child.

NITA. Why ever for?

RITA. An animal must be.

NITA. In a trap, perhaps.

RITA. Animal-like.

NITA. When they get that hungry, I suppose.

RITA. That's what I meant.

NITA. Civilization is but a veneer.

RITA. Why would anyone let their own child starve?

NITA. No one would, let, I suppose.

RITA. Not let, exactly.

NITA. It's complex.

RITA. Totally.

NITA. Allegiances, patronage, family.

RITA. Names difficult to pronounce.

NITA. One can't keep things straight in one's head.

RITA. Civil wars are the absolute worst.

NITA. So much suffering for what?

RITA. Would you like some oysters on the half-shell?

NITA. Moon Shoals and Kumamoto.

RITA. Afloat in their own juice.

NITA. So smooth sliding down the throat.

RITA. I don't think they cry like that.

NITA. Like what?

RITA. What we just heard.

NITA. A whimper, perhaps.

RITA. That's what I meant.

NITA. When they get weak.

RITA. Must have been an animal caught in a trap.

NITA. Unsettling, nevertheless.

RITA. They turn their heads; unclench their little fingers and toes.

NITA. That must be so terrible to watch.

RITA. Oh, my goodness. I could not watch that.

NITA. I turn the channel; that's what I do.

RITA. I meant if it were mine.

NITA. Yours?

RITA. Yes.

NITA. How could that be?

RITA. It couldn't, of course.

NITA. Well, that is a blessing, is it not?

RITA. How ever do such terrible things come to pass?

NITA. Much of the world's oil ships through the Bab al-Mandab strait.

RITA. Geography is destiny, do you agree?

NITA. Strategic link between the Indian Ocean and the Mediterranean Sea.

RITA. Gate of Tears, it's been called.

NITA. Strategic locations usually are. Troy was.

RITA. Please, try the baked bass.

NITA. Absolutely divine braised buttery sauce.

RITA. *Times* recipe. It's a proxy war.

NITA. The Saudis blockaded the ports.

RITA. It's not helpful to criticize the Saudis.

NITA. Quite right.

RITA. Saudi Arabia is our ally.

NITA. Delightful, this white Bordeaux.

RITA. We'll move to a red with the beef.

NITA. "Nobody makes what we make and now we're selling it all over the world."

RITA. Is that so?

NITA. I am quoting President Trump.

RITA. Whatever was *he* talking about?

NITA. Missile defense systems.

RITA. Such a comfort, they are.

NITA. The Houthis shot a missile at Saudi Arabia.

RITA. Iran gave it to them. That made everything worse.

NITA. Our missile defense system knocked their missile right out of the sky.

RITA. Well, of course, it did.

NITA. I'll take a piece of that roast beef.

RITA. Please.

NITA. Tender.

RITA. Grass-raised, organic.

NITA. If one is going to eat meat.

RITA. In moderation, our little sins.

NITA. No one in Saudi was hurt.

RITA. We can be thankful for that.

NITA. Please, I'll take another thin slice of the beef.

RITA. War with Iran.

NITA. Iran has had it coming quite some time.

RITA. Yemen imports most of its food.

NITA. They grow coffee, for export, and khat.

RITA. What is that?

NITA. Feel good drug.

RITA. I'm glad they have some escape.

NITA. Frankincense and myrrh, they used to grow.

RITA. How Biblical.

NITA. Medicinal, postpartum effects. Contract the womb. Clot the blood.

RITA. For Mary from the three Wise Men.

NITA. Khat, too, for Mary, do you suppose? [*They laugh.*]

RITA. The Saudis won't stop.

NITA. I suppose they think they have no choice.

RITA. As long as the Houthis, of course.

NITA. The Shiite Houthi.

RITA. Are they?

NITA. Zaidi, yes.

RITA. And the Saudis are Sunni.

NITA. Wahhabi. Wahhabis. Salafi.

RITA. They don't like the Houthi.

NITA. The Houthi rebelled.

RITA. The Houthi promised the people reforms.

NITA. The Houthi want what they can't have.

RITA. Al-Qaeda, of course, is taking advantage.

NITA. We've had to put boots on the ground.

RITA. That's not so. Is that so?

NITA. I suppose so. Green Berets.

RITA. Air strikes, I know about.

NITA. We are simply refueling their jets.

RITA. Made by us. I'm full up.

NITA. Me too.

RITA. They might have been civilians.

NITA. I hardly think so.

RITA. Yes, in the market, 52.

NITA. Precision instruments, first-rate intelligence.

RITA. A wedding party. More than one.

NITA. The area is thick with insurgents.

RITA. On the happiest day of one's life.

NITA. Was yours that?

RITA. No. Civilians in their beds.

NITA. They use civilians as human shields.

RITA. Barbarians.

NITA. He's a charmer, the Saudi prince, Mohammed bin Salman.

RITA. He let women drive. Such piercing black eyes.

NITA. I could not survive without my car.

RITA. The sewage system in Sana'a has stopped working.

NITA. The Saudis are in charge of the reconstruction.

RITA. That's only fair; rebuild what you bomb.

NITA. Billions to be made in the private sector.

RITA. This is an aged white rind goat cheese, from Spain.

NITA. Weapons sales are essential to growth.

RITA. Take just a taste.

NITA. 2.3 billion promised to us by the Prince.

RITA. It has the slightest peppery tang.

NITA. Follow up with this salted dark chocolate. My small contribution.

RITA. There's cholera everywhere.

NITA. Chocolate is good for digestion.

RITA. The United Nations fears mass starvation.

NITA. Don't get me started.

RITA. Just a small piece. Not terribly caloric.

NITA. On the United Nations.

RITA. Oh, yes, nobody likes them.

NITA. We had such great hopes.

RITA. For world peace.

NITA. World peace, yes.

RITA. We can still wish.

NITA. We still do, of course.

RITA. What a marvelous meal.

[*A terrible cry is heard.*]

END

AN AFTERWORD

By Lydia Koniordou

I first met Karen Malpede during an international forum on women in theater at the European Cultural Centre of Delphi. It was in the early '90s.

Directly after my presentation, I saw a Mediterranean-looking woman with short dark hair and bright brown eyes approaching me. She introduced herself and surprised me with a proposal to direct *Kassandra,* a novella by Christa Wolf, which she had adapted for her students at New York University's Tisch School of the Arts.

It felt utopian to me, but being in Delphi, where anything seemed possible, I answered without hesitation, "Why not?"

Sure enough, a year later (it must have been 1993), I found myself at NYU in Washington Square Park, intensely rehearsing a play of great power with her students. The performance that developed was a daring, poetic, sensitive anti-war experience, as seen from the eyes of women. It seemed to deeply affect the students and audience. I know that it had a deep effect on me personally.

Karen had dramatized the inner life of Kassandra, as Wolf records it in the unbroken monologue of her novella. The cast had three Kassandras: the doomed one in the chariot, the girl in defiance of her father, and the young woman, a vibrant anti-war activist. A chorus of more than 20 performers became the characters who had lived the events. Without betraying the spirit of Wolf, often in a sharp and startling manner, Karen had laid bare inner truths in the story.

At night Karen and I continued our work with endless discussions that included her husband, George Bartenieff, an amazing actor and exceptional personality. These talks — which were profound and so revelatory for me of the American artistic spirit that George and Karen knew so well, had experienced intimately — were the foundation of a lasting friendship. On the other side of the Atlantic Ocean, I had discovered a rare, human communication.

During my stay in New York, at the Theatre for the New City, George and Karen introduced me to the recent work of two artists who had been for me, as well as for many Greek artists, a great source of inspiration, especially in the years after the dictatorship when we all longed to make contact with movements of artistic freedom of expression.

They were Peter Schuman of the Bread and Puppet Theater and Judith Malina of the Living Theatre. Their work had changed the way we approached theater, and it certainly affected my work, both as an actor and director. The two were direct and vital lines to the avant-garde movement of American theater in the '60s and its contribution to new horizons along with that of European masters such as Peter Brook, Jerzy Grotowski, and later Eugenio Barba and Arianne Mnoushkin.

We are grateful to these artists because they have reminded us through their work, their lives, and the stand they took in society that art and theater are indispensable to conscious citizens of the world. In Athens, in the fifth century B.C., the cultivation of active consciousness in the audience was theater's reason for being. It stood as a third pillar together with democracy and freedom.

As artists and citizens of the world, Karen and George (who died in 2022) have tended this flame of freedom in their thought and work and shared it with grace and generosity in productions and performances, and with me whenever we met.

Quite recently, in 2023, we were united as artists again in Karen's wonderful play, *Troy Too,* that included, in little more than an hour — quite miraculously in my opinion — the recent experience of Black Lives Matter, Me Too, the pollution of the planet, and the pandemic. There was a very powerful free reference to the *Trojan Women* of

Euripides as background. I held the part of Hecuba — as a contemporary homeless woman.

This turned out to be an amazing production, deeply moving to all, an exceptional experience. The audience connected at once with the core of the play and expressed a warm and grateful response in their applause. I really hope we can reprise it in the future.

George Bartenieff was with us on tape, voicing his unique and last monologue as The Fish drowned by plastic.

Dear Karen, I am glad to have the opportunity to thank you publicly for your exceptional contribution to theater, for your strong voice in the service of freedom, and for your friendship.

I wish this book a "good sailing journey," as we say in Greece!

BIOGRAPHIES

KAREN MALPEDE is the author, and frequently the director, of 22 plays. With the actor-director-producer, George Bartenieff, she co-founded Theater Three Collaborative in 1995. She is author of the memoir *Last Radiance: Radical Lives, Bright Deaths* (Vine Leaves Press, 2025). Her recent plays are: *Troy Too* (HERE, 2023); *Blue Valiant* (Farm Arts Collective, YouTube, 2021); *Other Than We* (La MaMa, 2018, podcast for Columbia University's Earth Institute, 2019); *Extreme Whether* (La MaMa, 2016; ARTCOP21, Paris, 2015; Theater for the New City, 2014); *Dinner During Yemen,* (Signature Theater, New York, 2018); *Hermes in the Anthropocene: A Dogologue* (University of Iowa, Iowa City, 2019; Reed College, Portland, 2015); *The Beekeeper's Daughter* (Theater for the New City, New York, 2016; Theater Row Theater, 1996; Bleeker Street Theater, 1995; *Dionysus Festival,* Italy, 1994); *Another Life (Art of Justice Festival,* Gerald W. Lynch Theater, September 11, 2011; Irondale, 2012; Theater for the New City, 2013; Guild Hall, London, 2013); *Iraq: Speaking of War* (CUNY–Graduate Center, New York, 2006; Culture Project, New York, 2007). With George Bartenieff, she co-adapted and directed *I Will Bear Witness,* (Obie Award, Classic Stage, 2000; New End Theatre, London; English Theatre, Berlin; Theater J tour, Germany and Austria 2001–2005). She is author of the anthology *Plays in Time: The Beekeeper's Daughter, Prophecy, Another Life, Extreme Whether* (Intellect, 2016); editor of *Acts of War: Iraq and Afghanistan in Seven Plays* (Northwestern, 2011), and author of an anthology of her early work *A Monster Has Stolen the Sun and Other Plays.* Her short plays, fiction, and essays on ecofeminism, the climate crisis, a new green Federal Theater, bearing witness, the Iraq war, and the U.S. torture program, have been published in *The Kenyon*

Review, TriQuarterly, Dark Matter, Howlround, Transformations, Torture Magazine, New Theater Quarterly, TDR, New York Times, and elsewhere. She has taught theater and literature at Smith College, New York University Tisch School of the Arts, and John Jay College–CUNY.

MARVIN CARLSON is the Sidney E. Cohn Distinguished Professor of Theatre, Comparative Literature, and Middle Eastern Studies, The Graduate Center, The City University of New York. His wide-ranging research and teaching interests include dramatic theory and Western European theater history, dramatic literature and translation, especially of the 18th, 19th, and 20th centuries. He has been awarded the ATHE Career Achievement Award, the George Jean Nathan Prize, the Bernard Hewitt prize, the George Freedley Award, and a Guggenheim Fellowship. He has been a Walker-Ames Professor at the University of Washington, a fellow of the Institute for Advanced Studies at Indiana University, a visiting professor at the Freie Universität of Berlin, and a Fellow of the American Theatre. In 2005 he was awarded an honorary doctorate by the University of Athens. His best-known book, *Theories of the Theatre,* has been translated into eight languages. His book, *The Haunted Stage,* won the Calloway Prize.

LYDIA KONIORDOU was born in Athens, studied English literature at the University of Athens, and graduated from the National Theater Drama School, in combination with parallel studies in music and dance. As an actress, she has interpreted major roles, both classical and contemporary, in Greece and abroad, collaborating with the National Theater, the Karolos Koun Art Theater, the Municipal Theaters of Larissa, Volos, and Patras, as well as with the Chatelet Theater in Paris, Teatro Piccolo in Milan, and many others. She has worked with eminent theater directors such as Karolos Koun, Alexis Minotis,

Kostas Tsianos, Lefteris Voyatzis, Sotiris Chatzakis, Robert Wilson, Alexander Vassiliev, Yannis Kokkos, and others. As a director, besides contemporary plays, she staged many ancient Greek tragedies for the National Theater, the Municipal Theaters of Larissa and Volos, the Athens Conservatory, and the Getty Museum in California. For her work and overall contribution in this field, she has been awarded the Karolos Koun and the Critics awards. She has served as artistic director of the Municipal Theaters of Volos and Patras. Koniordou served as the Minister of Culture and Sports of the Hellenic Republic from November 5, 2016 to August 29, 2018.